EFFECTIVE LEARNING

EFFECTIVE LEARNING

A Four-Step Strategy

ROBERT C. BELL

PALMETTO
P U B L I S H I N G
Charleston, SC
www.PalmettoPublishing.com

Effective Learning
Copyright © 2024 by Robert C. Bell

First Edition

Paperback ISBN: 979-8-8229-4095-6
eBook ISBN: 979-8-8229-4096-3

To my senior-year, Irondequoit NY high school English teacher, John Williamson, who made us write an essay *every* week and then spent many hours of his time correcting each little error. I wasn't mature enough to thank him at the time, but he provided the foundation for me being able to have a successful career and to write this book. For him, I can only express my appreciation posthumously. Yet, for those teachers who currently sacrifice their time to make similar extra efforts that can change the lives of their students, I also dedicate this book.

CONTENTS

INTRODUCTION

With shelves full of how-to-learn books, many with great improvement ideas, why another book? Two reasons.

The first is that, unlike most authors, I know what it's like to be a struggling student. As a disinterested, lousy student early on and later as a hard working student with inadequate learning skills, I know how far the typical lower-achieving student can be from having a worthwhile learning strategy. And, unlike authors who were themselves excellent students, I believe I understand and can communicate better with students performing at a non-excellent level.

I had a poor start. My parents never read to me, we didn't go to museums or other educational places, and I lacked what's now called "cultural enrichment." Consequently, when my first-grade teacher divided us into above-average, average, and below-average groups, I accepted the fact that I was in the last group. It didn't help that later we moved every couple of years when I was in elementary and middle school.

I got Cs and Ds, repeated fourth grade, and had little interest in school. It wasn't until high school that I began to get serious about studying. However, I didn't then magically develop a good learning strategy. I just greatly increased the number of hours I studied in an inefficient way. Fortunately, even with this lack of efficiency, the amount of hard work I put in enabled me to improve my grades just enough to go to college. Without an effective study strategy, though, I never used my time well. I was always disadvantaged by having inferior study skills. If only I'd had a book like this!

The second reason I wrote this book is that most instructions in typical how-to-learn books are difficult to remember and act upon because they aren't part of any overall learning strategy. I remember one book that introduced a whooping two-page list of 21 bulleted recommendations simply by saying here are some major learning tips. They were good, but I don't remember any of them because they weren't organized in any particular way. Our brains don't easily store memories of random bits of information. Learning tips should be meaningfully integrated into a coherent plan for studying.

That's why the subtitle of *Effective Learning* is *A Basic Four-Step Study Strategy*. Reflecting on what I could have done better as a student and doing years of related research, I've created this short book containing what I wished I'd developed earlier for myself: a *basic* strategy, a logical plan for learning.

Here's a quick preview of the four steps.

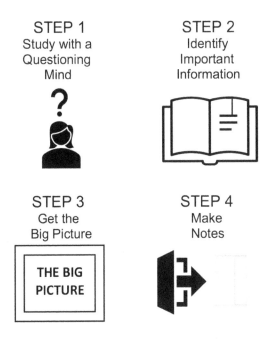

STEP 1
Study with a
Questioning
Mind

STEP 2
Identify
Important
Information

STEP 3
Get the
Big Picture

STEP 4
Make
Notes

I explain the theories behind the four-step strategy, but you don't have to recall them when you're studying. Nor do you need to remember a long list of tips. Just by using the four steps, you'll study in about the same way you would have if you'd bothered to memorize, recall, and act upon pages and pages of individual pieces of advice. You'll be able to maximize the learning you get out of each hour of studying and become a first-class student.

PART 1:
FOLLOW A FOUR-STEP LEARNING STRATEGY

CHAPTER 1
THINK ABOUT YOUR CURRENT LEARNING STRATEGY

Learning to learn is life's most important skill.
~ Tony Buzon (Learning expert & inventor of Mind Maps)

<u>Understand Why It's Critical to Develop a Strategy</u>

You probably do what most students do—which is to follow the typical, poor study "strategy" summarized below.

TYPICAL STUDY STRATEGY

1. Read and highlight what seems to be important;

2. Close the book or program and go on to the next assignment;

3. Take some notes in class; and

4. Review, just before the exam, the highlighter material and maybe some class notes.

This approach is not surprising. In school, you're "taught what to learn, what to think, and what to remember. But there are few if any classes on *how* to learn, *how* to think, and *how* to remember."[1]

You only pick up bits of how-to-learn knowledge as you go along, and even most college students lack good study skills.[2]

This typical "strategy" produces only superficial (that means sketchy) learning when you actually study. Then you forget most of what of what little you learned between your initial studying and returning for pre-exam reviewing. Often, that reviewing turns out to be only a rushed re-learning of what you've largely forgotten. You jam a few last-minute pieces of information into your head—not enough to do well on the exam nor to retain anything afterwards.

The key to improving what you learn? **Don't just jump in, quickly read, and then leave it**!

Instead, have a sound learning strategy that guides you through the highly valuable work you can do before, during, and after reading. That will help you learn better, remember more, and get outstanding results.

Just as mechanics and carpenters do their work well only by possessing and knowing how to use the right tools, so too it is with studying.

Similarly, just as some people are better with mechanical things or woodworking, some—at first anyway—are better at reading, writing, and math: the major school skills. If you're not one of them, you can still become a superior learner if you have an effective strategy and are willing to study more *initially* than those who currently find schoolwork easier.

Although you can modify this book's approach to whatever works best for you, the four strategy steps to be described in the next short chapters should serve you well.

Combine Your Strategy with a Strong Effort

Your strategy must be accompanied by a steady determination to do the related work. How well you learn largely reflects the effort you alone make. Ideally, you'd have a great school, some excellent teachers, and a supportive home life. Lacking any of these will make things more difficult, but won't prevent you from becoming a high achiever.

Follow the advice of a person who had a low-income single mother and two siblings, lived in areas full of drugs and killings, and attended inferior schools:

I know the struggle, but I'm so thankful that I didn't let that determine who I was going to be in life. . . . If you are struggling right now, let your circumstances and surroundings motivate you to do better. You've got to push forward and make something of yourself, no matter what. Study hard now and play later. Get your education and keep your dreams alive.[3]

At this time, one of the best things you can do for your future is to become a successful student. Do that by combining an effective strategy with a powerful determination to learn.

Without a good strategy, increased effort alone will bring only a small amount of improvement. To be truly successful, you need to know what you're doing by having a useful strategy to guide your hard work.

Strong Effort + Poor Strategy $\Longrightarrow$ Some Success

Strong Effort + Good Strategy $\Longrightarrow$ Great Success

The next four chapters will provide the good strategy you need.

CHAPTER 2
STUDY WITH A QUESTIONING MIND
(STEP 1)

Try to understand the following paragraph:

> The procedure is actually quite simple. First you arrange things into different groups. Of course, one pile may be sufficient depending on how much there is to do. . . . At first, the whole procedure will seem complicated. Soon, however, it will just become another facet of life. It is difficult to foresee any end to the necessity for this task in the immediate future, but then one can never tell. After the procedure is completed, one arranges the material into different groups again. Then they can be put into their appropriate places. Eventually, they will be used once more, and the whole cycle will then have to be repeated.[4]

Confused? Probably. But what if, before you started reading, you had taken a quick look at the material that included the above description and seen a reference to washing of clothes. Then the paragraph would have made sense.

This is an exaggerated example of what you encounter when you begin an assignment that you don't know much or anything about. Most of what you read first won't make much sense.

Let's pretend, for example, that you're a typical student, and your homework includes a chapter on the causes of World War I or on instructions on how to solve an algebra problem. What's your first step? Duh! Open the book or program and start reading. What do you want to learn? Again duh! The causes of World War I or how to solve the algebra problem. Why do you want to learn those things? Double duh! For the test.

You begin reading, hoping the study material will somehow indicate what you need to know. Your goals are vague aside from learning for the test. Thus, all of your study material will have essentially the same value.[5] You'll tend to read everything at the same speed, have trouble remembering, and be easily distracted.[6]

Here's an important idea that will help you with these problems. *Don't dive into your studying without having ideas, questions, about what might be good to know.*[7] While you may start reading with only a few questions, you can add to them as you continue studying.

Take a few minutes before beginning every assignment to think about what questions you might have about the study material.

Creating questions is as important as answering them, if not more so, because framing good questions focuses your attention on the right issues.[8]

How do you come up with questions? Not hard. You can do that mostly by:

- Thinking for a couple of minutes about how the reading material might relate to what else you're studying in the course or to some personal interest.[9]

- Pre-reading the assigned text—skimming over what you'll read, looking especially at information like:
  o "Titles and headings;
  o Opening paragraphs/introductions;
  o Summary paragraphs/lists of key Points;
  o Bold, italicized, underlined, or highlighted words/phrases; and
  o Visual information (graphs, maps, tables, pictures.)"[10]

- Thinking skeptically (suspiciously) as you read. Always be asking yourself whether what you're reading makes sense, is true, or could be presented more effectively. Don't just automatically suck it all up; be questioning.

What benefits do you get from coming up with questions?

- Seeking answers to questions increases your level of interest. "The human brain simply can't resist a good question. We are problem-solving machines. Questions, therefore, cause our brains to fire up and pay attention unlike anything else." [11] Compare that to your attitude when you have no pre-reading questions.

- When looking at the study material to develop questions, you learn about what's coming up. That helps you begin to understanding earlier and more deeply, unlike being clueless like you were with the washing clothes paragraph.

- If you're studying with unanswered questions in mind, once you find the answers, you'll remember them better than you would have if you just saw the answers when they came up in your reading.[12]

Pre-thinking before you begin studying and staying alert for further questions as you read will take a little extra time, but you'll save more time overall. You'll have an improved sense of what you're looking for and an idea of the whole and how the parts fit together. You'll also gain a substantially improved understanding and a heightened alertness that will enable you to get more out of what you read.

The *big picture* on the next page summarizes the essence of this chapter. Getting the big picture is strategy step 3 to be discussed in chapter 4, but starting to provide big pictures with this chapter will give you an idea of their nature and usefulness.

THE BIG PICTURE for Ch. 2.

I never thought about reading ahead before starting an assignment. I would just begin reading and look for things that might be on a test. With that as my only goal, I can now see that I'll tend to be bored and gain only a superficial, easy-to-forget idea of the material.

I can do better by first taking a few minutes to skim the reading material, glancing at section titles, tables/graphs, and a few sentences here and there. Usually that small effort will:
- ✓ Create questions for which I'd seek answers, thereby increasing my interest and keeping me more alert and focused;
- ✓ Improve my memory of the material when I find answers to my pre-reading questions, which will be more meaningful to me because I personally sought those answers;
- ✓ Make the study material more understandable since I'll have a better idea of how what I read early on fits into the whole assignment

I'll also benefit from thinking how the study material relates to what else I'm learning in the course, how it might be of personal interest, and whether it makes sense. This will require only a little bit of time and can make me a more effective learner.

CHAPTER 3
IDENTIFY IMPORTANT INFORMATION (STEP 2)

This is just a sample page to illustrate highlighting. And this first paragraph is just to have a couple of sentences at the top of the page to highlight.

Recalling something you learned just minutes or hours ago is of little value. It's fresh in your mind, easy to retrieve. You confidently say: "Yes, I've got this."[1] Oh yeah. What if you wait days or weeks during which you throw many other thoughts into your brain? Then, can you find that memory, or have you partially or totally forgotten it?

When you do spaced repetition, you have to make serious efforts to remember what you partially forgot after each space away from your study material. That struggling to remember something gets it firmer into your brain and more readily retrieved later.

Spaced learning also increases your understanding. By watching a movie more than once, you see things you didn't notice before. Repeating study material is the same. Your brain sees new things and what you recognized earlier in new ways.

How long should the learning spaces be? You want enough time between study episodes to experience some forgetting, and remembering becomes at least somewhat effortful. It's that effort that reinforces learning. Yet don't wait too long. You want to do retrieval, not re-learning.

This is how ⇐ most students mark important parts of what they're reading (if they can mark their books). Perhaps you don't mark at all, believing you can remember what's essential. You can't, and you should mark important material. Highlighting, however, is not the way to go, as explained below.

"Distinguishing the important from the unimportant information arguably is the most critical skill in successful studying." [13] If you become overloaded with both important and unimportant information, you'll have trouble understanding and remembering.

Thus, as you read, you should identify as best you can what is most important. Because you can't keep much of what you study in your head, you then need an effective way to record answers to your questions and other key information.

So why not do that by highlighting? The reason is that some of what you thought was essential as you read along might no longer seem to be useful in light of what you know after reading a whole chapter or article. But you already highlighted that information. How do you erase it?" Well, . . . you can't. That's the problem with using a marker. You wanted to mark only important sentences, but now you're also stuck with a lot of colored, less important stuff.

To decide what's important with what you know *after* completing your reading, you need a way to record what you *initially* believe is important that allows you to erase *later* what then seems to be less important.

Using penciled brackets and lines is one useful method for ultimately recording only the key information.

1. Bracket/Line Important Material

Your good friend is the pencil, not the highlighter, even though you can't always use it because some of your work is done on electronic devices.

Nevertheless, you can use brackets and lines with some of your material, and the technique itself illustrates how to record the essential information everywhere in an effective way. That is, by marking:

a. What *might be important* as you first read;

b. What, after you finish reading, you then consider to be *definitely important*; and

c. Which information is *highly important*.

We'll go over the technique for markable books and then explain what to do with unmarkable and electronic material.

As you read, begin by putting erasable ⌐
backets by sentences you think might be
important. Again, don't use a highlighter
or a pen because you may want to erase
some marked material later. ⌐

Don't underline as you read because that might require a messy erasing job later.

After completing an assignment, review your bracketed material in view of what you then know and determine what you believe is definitely important. Erase brackets around information you now think simply isn't that important. Also, since some bracketed information might be better expressed elsewhere, erase brackets around inferior sentences. Finally, you might add new brackets when you see a need for more explanatory information.

Then <u>connect the brackets with vertical lines if you think a whole passage is important</u> and now is the time to <u>underline highly important sentences</u>.

In summary:

<table>
<tr><td>Maybe Important</td><td>Important</td></tr>
<tr><td>Once you think you have the essential information bracketed, connect each pair of brackets with a solid, vertical line if you believe the material is important; and underline sentences you see as being very important. Only when you have a good idea of what's important should you underline.</td><td>Once you think you have the essential information bracketed, connect each pair of brackets with a solid, vertical line if you believe the material is important; and underline sentences you see as being very important. Only when you have a good idea of what's important should you underline.</td></tr>
</table>

Very Important

<u>Once you think you have the essential information bracketed, connect each pair of brackets with a solid, vertical line if you believe the material is important;</u> and underline sentences you see as being very important. Only when you have a good idea of what's important should you underline.

Also note that there are ways to mark important material other than by using the just-described bracketing method. For example, one learning expert believes that:

The simplest way of marking the [important] passages is to draw a line beside them. If the passage is especially important, draw a double line beside it. Use an interrogation mark beside points that you are not sure about, or where you wish to make further inquiries.[14]

You may even come up with another approach. That's fine as long as your markings can be deleted after you finish reading.

While this book's general approach is most useful when you need to pick out key information from lengthy material, like in a history book, it's also useful for STEM (Science, Technology, Engineering, and Math) subjects, which have a ton of required information on each page. Be aware, however, that STEM material is often written in a way that bracketing alone cannot neatly capture the key information. In those cases you'll need to carefully pick out and meaningfully rearrange that information later when making notes (strategy step 4).

When you can't mark up your physical study material, use lightly penciled brackets and erase them later. And you don't add vertical lines or underlying. Instead, you can put comments on sticky notes or sheets of paper.[15]

2. Use Equivalent Technique for Electronic Material

While having some of your education delivered digitally has advantages, it means your marking system won't have handwritten brackets and lines. In that regard, note that the don't-use-a-highlighter advice relates largely to the erasing problem. With e-books, on the other hand, the simplest option might be to use highlighting, which can be easily removed. *Thus, deleting unnecessary highlighting on electronic devices is the equivalent of erasing brackets in physical books.* The objective is the same, which is not to go overboard with your marking. "Those who just confidently turn their reading material into a work of modern art by merrily highlighting anything that seems vaguely relevant do not benefit from the process."[16]

In summary, depending on the material, you'll have somewhat different information-recording approaches. They'll look roughly like this:

Markable Physical Material

Finally, you might add new brackets when you see a need for more explanatory information. Once you think you have the essential information bracketed, <u>connect each pair of brackets with a solid, vertical line if you believe the material is important; and underline sentences you see as being very important</u>.

Use full bracketing and lining.

Non-Markable Physical Material

Finally, you might add new brackets when you see a need for more explanatory information. Once you think you have the essential information bracketed, connect each pair of brackets with a solid, vertical line if you believe the material is important; and underline sentences you see as being very important.

Use light pencil brackets; erase after making notes.

Electronic Material

Finally, you might add new brackets when you see a need for more explanatory information. Once you think you have the essential information bracketed, connect each pair of brackets with a solid, vertical line if you believe the material is important; and underline sentences you see as being very important.

After reading, keep highlighting only on the most important information.

By using one of these techniques, you record the key information and leave out the less-important bits. You also review and think about what you marked, which improves your understanding and ability to remember your study material. Yet, if you stop now and assume you can just go back later to do a pre-exam review of your bracketed information, you'll be insufficiently prepared for that exam—although better prepared than if you used only the typical student's study strategy of reading and leaving. There are two more steps coming up that will help you greatly.

THE BIG PICTURE for Ch. 3

If I mark and leave what I initially thought was important with no further thinking, I'll have too much marked, a poor understanding, and a short-term memory of it. Instead, I should review and think about what I marked after I finish reading in light of what I then know.

I need to use a method that allows me to erase markings of what, after finishing an assignment, I then believe is not that important or is better expressed elsewhere. Bracketing and lining is one such method. The thinking involved in reviewing the bracketed information will improve my understanding; revising will produce a smaller, more manageable amount of marked information; and looking at the material a second time will improve my memory of it.

CHAPTER 4
GET THE BIG PICTURE (STEP 3)

After marking important information in step 2, you still have a number of unconnected pieces of information that could quickly blow away like leaves of a tree in the fall.

When reading an assignment, sometimes you just felt that something was valuable and should get a bracket. Or you saw a good summary paragraph that merited being marked. Then too, if sentences were bolded or italicized, you probably put brackets around them. You also marked information that answered questions you had. That whole process could have produced a fairly good record of what was most important.

And then, by thinking about what was most essential *after* you read, you not ended up with only the most important information marked, but you also increased your knowledge beyond what a typical student gains only by highlighting and quickly moving on to the next assignment.

That's excellent, but at this stage you still have only a bunch of marked pieces of information. Think of those pieces as the dots in the brain to the left. They're mostly unconnected. See how there aren't lines between most of them? They're not linked in your mind in a way that creates good understanding, and isolated pieces are hard to remember. Thus, your grasp of the information is still weak.

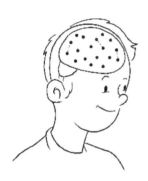

A useful further step, therefore, is to take a few minutes to connect some of the major pieces in your brain by creating a *big picture*.

What's that? If someone were to ask you to briefly describe what you just read, what you got out of it, your answer would be an example of a big picture. Flip back two pages and take a look at the big picture. It summarized *what you read* and *why it was valuable*. That's a big picture.

By developing a big picture, you can pull some of the most critical pieces together in a meaningful way.[17] And the thinking you do in the process will help check on how well you understood the material

The issue is that "you can't really know anything if you just remember isolated facts and try to bang 'em back." [18] A big picture is an *initial* way to bring isolated facts together in a simple, sensible manner. There are two major ways to do that.

1. Zero In on Basic, Essential Information

If you can't explain it simply, you don't understand it well enough. [19]
~ Albert Einstein

Seeing something in its simplest form means getting to the key parts—the main points—and dropping unneeded details.

Simple can be harder than complex. You must work hard to get your thinking clean to make it simple. But it's worth it in the end because once you get there, you can move mountains. [20]
~ Steve Jobs

Although some study material is already in the simplest form, such as a vocabulary word, most is more complicated and should be boiled down to what's most essential. And what is most *essential* tends to be what is *fundamental* for understanding.

Let's say that you landed from Mars and picked up a book of baseball rules. You discover rules for foul balls, walking a batter, etc. Yet, you don't know how the basic game is played. How meaningful would those rules be? Get the basics down first. Then the smaller points make sense.

> If you're going to spend the time, you should be rewarded for your effort, but only if you get the 'big picture' . . . . If you spend 10 hours focused on the tiny details but don't know where they stem from or how they all connect, that's a waste of time.[21]

By determining what is most essential, you don't leave your assignments with just a bunch of soon-to-be-forgotten details in your head. Instead, you 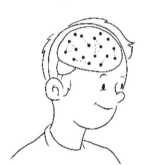 know the simple essence of what you read. You connected some important but isolated bits of information to each other in meaningful ways.

You might be saying to yourself: "How can writing a few sentences really help me better understand and remember the 20-page chapter I just read?" The answer is that what actually helps is the thinking you do to be able to write those sentences. You have to go back to summarize and make sense of the study material. You think about the major points and how they linked to each other. That's an important learning step.

2. Use Pretend Teaching to Help See the Big Picture

Another effective way to help create a big picture is to use pretend teaching. Trying to explain what

you think you've learned to someone else—even a pretend person—helps you get to the core of the material, as well as points out gaps in your knowledge. Pretending to teach forces you to spell out what you've learned—to put the pieces together in a sensible way. When you're trying to teach, kind-of/sort-of knowing doesn't work.

> Have you ever found yourself explaining something you thought you totally understood only to discover, in the midst of your explanation, that you were still confused about some part of it? If you hadn't been explaining the information to someone else, then when do you think you would have realized you didn't completely understand the information?[22]

Note that pretend teaching can be used at any stage of your studying, not just to create big pictures.

THE BIG PICTURE for Ch. 4

A big picture is a short explanation of what I learned. It provides a framework for bringing some of the major pieces of information together in a way that makes sense to me and helps prevent the material from quickly fading away from my memory. It doesn't take long to do, and it can improve my understanding in addition to my memory.

For example, I could have finished reading a history chapter, marked a bunch of separate bits of apparently important information, and then moved on to do a math assignment. If I do a big picture before starting on the math, I can tie the bits of history knowledge together in a more understandable, meaningful way that will stick in my mind and not be crowded out by the fresher math information.

The two main ways to develop a big picture are to break down what I learned into a simple summary and to use pretend teaching. Both of these help produce a big picture because they force me to come up with a simplified, clear, explanation of what I studied.

CHAPTER 5
MAKE NOTES (STEP 4)

By using brackets or something similar, you marked the important information (step 2), and you did a big picture (step 3), but in terms of understanding you're still skimming along on the surface of your study material. Furthermore, your memory of that will still be fragile. If you want to fully understand, retain, and be able to use such information in the future, you need to give it some more thought and put it into your mind in a way that's most meaningful to you, using your own words.

You might believe you've accomplished enough by doing strategy steps 1-3. Besides, with several homework assignments each night, where will you find time to make notes? Often, in fact, you won't have enough time to do all four strategy steps at roughly the same time for each subject. You might need to put off note-making until the weekend or some other day. That's OK. Still, its hugely important that you do make notes when you can. Yes, that will take extra time. The real waste of time, though, would be to do strategy steps 1-3 and then the stop. You'd be left with knowledge gaps and a still-weak memory. [23]

When studying, you largely follow an author's vocabulary and thoughts. If, however, you can't explain the material in your own words and in a way that's meaningful to you, you'll have an incomplete understanding and poor memory of it.

Those considered to be 'Great Brains' in the fields of art, science, politics, literature, the military, business, and education have all used notes to help them think.[24]
~ Tony Buzan (Learning expert & Mind Maps inventor)

So what do you put in your notes? You might have heard that it's a good idea to put everything that might be on the exam in your notes. WRONG! You can only remember so much. If you overload yourself, you'll spend valuable time on details you'll probably forget, and you'll have less time for the most important information. Making notes is about writing out, in your own words, the key points and the essential supporting information in a manner that makes sense to you personally.

1. Use Your Own Words and Way

We tend to think we understand what we read— until we try to rewrite it in our own words."[25] You _take_ notes by writing down words from the text, usually in the order the author presented them. Alas, that only copies "someone else's thoughts, as expressed in a book, article, or lecture," and you learn little.[26] You _make_ notes by using your own words and organizing them in a way that's most relevant for you.[27]

The ultimate advantage of taking notes is that they customize the information you need to retain to your vocabulary and your mode of thinking. At their best, notes allow you to organize and process information in a way that makes it most likely that you can use this information afterward.[28]

The chief value of note-making comes from the thinking you do in the process. "The *act* of notetaking is more important than the result."[29] It "pushes us to ask ourselves a series of questions: What's important? How can we rephrase this idea?" Such questions highlight the most valuable ideas and make them more meaningful.[30]

Most student fail to adequately think about their study material. As one college professor noted:

> My students who don't do very well think that 'keeping up' in a course means attending lectures and completing the reading on time. It's not until they prepare for an exam that they really think about what all the content means, try to organize it, and try fill gaps in their understanding. That is dangerously late to undertake that work. Worse, some of my struggling students don't even work on understanding at that point; they just start trying to memorize.[31]

You won't find yourself unprepared like that if you make notes in your own words and way. While there's no set formula for note-making, you can begin to organize your notes with a summary statement of what you're going to say, such as your big picture, and use the subsequent paragraphs to explain the main points and to connect the facts— all in a way that's meaningful for you.

Your notes will differ from subject to subject. With a math problem or a scientific process, for example, the emphasis might be on fully understanding and writing down each step needed to solve the problem or carry out the process. For history-course material or a novel, the focus would be more on understanding the major themes. Whatever the subject, your notes will seldom be much longer than one page for a single assignment.

Importantly too, take a critical look at the material you're making notes on. Do you agree or disagree with it? Do you think it could be approached in a more creative, useful way? Are there flaws in it? By critically evaluating what you're studying, you'll end up understanding it better and remembering it longer. Get out of the poor habit of simply recording the study material like some unthinking, electronic machine.

You may be saying to yourself: "I could do that questioning for some courses, but not for others like math, science, or foreign languages. For those courses the information is what it is. But is it presented in an ineffective way that you might be able to improve so you can understand it better? Or does it seem that a piece of information is missing, which can happen with expert authors who forget some of the information that new learners need? No matter what the course is, casting a critical eye on the study material and trying to be creative can be greatly beneficial.

Be aware also that your style of notes will vary greatly from subject to subject. Making notes on STEM subjects, for example, will focus mostly on concepts, formulas, and definitions. For literature you'll chiefly be concerned with knowing the plot, characters, and themes. While themes are also essential for history notes, events and their effects are needed too. Whatever the subject, the key is to focus on the important points.

2. <u>Make Notes Readable & Meaningful</u>

While electronic devices produce the most readable notes, handwritten ones are superior.  They make it easier to add diagrams and illustrations.[32] They involve more thinking than when you're typing.[33] And, by not using a laptop or tablet, you avoid the temptation to go off to your email, social media, and other distractions.[34]

Also, try printing by hand. You can print quickly; it's relatively easy to read; and it helps the information stick in your head, whereas typing doesn't.[35]

3. Try to Go Beyond Just Words.

Notes of Albert Einstein and Leonardo da Vinci and other creative geniuses used pictures, diagrams, colors, etc. In fact, in da Vinci's notes, "the diagrams and drawings are the focal points, not the words." [36] They helped him better see relationships that he might otherwise have missed. Drawings enrich understanding and are more interesting and easier to remember than lines of words. [37] So include some if they might be helpful. You don't need to be an artist.

4. Integrate Homework, Class, and Other Notes

When making reading notes, leave a margin of space about two inches wide on the right side of each page. When you learn more from classes (or outside sources) insert that information next to the

Reading Notes	O t h e r N o t e s

most closely related reading notes. You also can insert questions that you might want to research or bring up in class. That last point is especially important. Use your class time to clarify what you couldn't figure out from your homework.[38]

Keep in mind that when taking class notes, your brain can't process a lot of rapidly delivered new information. You'll only have time to capture major points, with any deep thinking waiting until later. Otherwise, you'll be distracted from catching the next important information.[39] (See Appendix C for abbreviations that can help speed up your notetaking.)

While in class, look for clues about what are the key points. For example, anything the teacher believes is useful enough to write on the board is worth noting. So too is information the teacher takes time to repeat. You can even get clues from the teacher's way of speaking (e.g., raised voice, slowed down to be extra clear, paused as if waiting for you to write something down) or body language (e.g., waving hands for emphasis).[40] Stay alert to all of these. Note also that teachers often provide a summary of what they're going to talk about before going into the details. That's something valuable you'll miss if you're not paying full attention at the beginning of the class.[41]

To reduce how much class material is new, try to go over related material before class. You won't always know what's going to be discussed, but if you have any class-related material, read it over. The more you can read about before class, the more easily you can follow what's being said and only need notes on what you didn't already learn.

After class, try to review your notes within 24 hours. Your memory fades quickly, making it increasingly difficult to make sense of what you hastily wrote.[42] Take your scribbled notes and, in a more readable form, put them into appropriate margin spaces with your reading notes.

If you have time, you could later integrate reading, class, and other notes into one rewritten document. That would get all the notes together in a superior way, provide valuable repetition to help you retain the material, and could highlight knowledge gaps.[43] Yes, you usually will lack time to do that, but when you can, you'll benefit significantly.

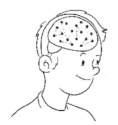

With the thinking involved with your note-making, you'll advance your understanding tremendously. In addition, the many new links you make in your brain between you previous knowledge and the new information will help you remember what you've learned.

THE BIG PICTURE for Ch. 5

By doing the first three strategy steps, I might believe I've got it. But I don't own it. I mostly just put into my head what an author said, without enough thinking. Only by using my own words in a way that's meaningful to me can I thoroughly understand and remember the information well.

In addition, I need to take good class notes, which will be easier if I can read something beforehand about what the teacher will discuss. Also, hand-printed notes, using more than just words (pictures, diagrams, etc.) , is the best way to go.

CHAPTER 6

UNDERSTAND THE TIMING AND VARIATIONS OF THE STRATEGY STEPS

Go through the four steps for a few weeks, and they'll come to you automatically. In the process, you'll become a much, much improved learner.

Two things should be clear by now:

- o Reading/marking once and then going on to a different assignment will leave you with only a poor understanding and ability to remember the material.

- o Each of the four strategy steps has substantial value.

Nevertheless, by now, you may have some concerns about the actual application of the 1-2-3-4 strategy as presented in the previous pages. Three major concerns may be:

--What happens if I can't do the four steps in the same time period?

--What if there are occasions when I never have enough time to do all four steps?

--What if the four-step strategy doesn't seem to be appropriate for the subject matter I'm studying?

1. <u>What happens if can't do the four steps in the same time period</u>?

When you study many subjects in one evening, you'll sometimes lack time for all the strategy steps. You might even have to wait several days to finish. That's OK, as long as you *do* complete all the steps.

One danger of not doing them together is that the longer you delay, the greater the chance you'll never finish. A second danger is that you'll leave the material, at least temporarily, without the fuller and more accurate understanding that doing the four steps together would have given you. Carrying that possibly deficient understanding in your mind for a time could affect how you incorrectly remember in the long term. So try to complete all the steps soon as possible

2. <u>What if there are occasions when I never have time to do all four steps</u>?

That will happen, especially with the more time-consuming step 4. The preliminary skimming and thinking of questions (step 1) should take only a few minutes. Marking and time spent reviewing and thinking about what you marked (step 2) will take longer, but not very long. And developing a Big Picture (step 3) takes only a short time. Thus, try to do at least those three steps. That will put you ahead of where you would have been without that work.

Realize, however, that if you don't go through the effort to make notes in your own words and way, you'll generally fall short of fully understanding your study material. You'll also miss an opportunity to look at the information from a different perspective and experience memory-enhancing repetition. So, again, try to make notes as soon as you can, even if time constraints only allow you to do a shorter version of what you'd ideally do.

3. <u>What if the four-step strategy doesn't seem to be appropriate for the subject matter I'm studying?</u>

This is a critical question. After all, where is the big picture when you're dealing with foreign language vocabulary words? What do you bracket when you're memorizing scientific terms, all of which you must learn? For those and similar cases, you'll need to develop your own learning strategies, although you'll probably use parts of the four steps, maybe in somewhat different ways.

Take, for example, a math-book chapter that explains how to solve a particular problem. It has so much essential information that bracketing is only marginally useful for separating important from less-important instructions. Making notes, on the other hand, is exceptionally beneficial. You don't want to do your math homework by trial and error, looking back at the chapter's model problem to get clues on how to proceed and ending up with only a vague idea of how you solved the problem. Instead, in your own words and way, you want to write down the concepts and procedures you used so you'll know how to apply them to solve that type of problem in the future.

Similarly, while you can use brackets on a novel you're reading, the number and nature of what you bracket would be much different than if you were applying step 2 to, say, a history book, which would follow the general pattern described earlier. For the novel, you'll mark only a small amount of information about characters, events, and relationships you might want to look back at when you're writing your notes. Furthermore, with a novel, you wouldn't do much after-reading reviewing and revising of bracketed information.

Thus, although you can usually apply the four strategy steps described in the preceding chapters, at times some will not be very useful or will need to be modified. For everything you study, however, you must go beyond the typical student strategy of simply reading the material and leaving it. Use your imagination to learn in ways that work best for you.

THE BIG PICTURE for Ch. 6

By doing the four strategy steps, I greatly increase my learning. I don't always need to do all four steps in the same time period, and there will be times when I can't even finish all the steps. Yet, the four steps make up a hugely beneficial package that I should try to complete whenever possible.

For almost any study material, doing step 1 is useful. Depending on the nature of my study material, however, steps 2-4 might be only of small value or will need to be modified. Then, I must develop a subject-specific strategy.

PART 2:
IMPROVE YOUR
STRATEGY EXECUTION

CHAPTER 7
FOCUS SMARTLY

You can be more effective with implementing your strategy *and* save time by smart focusing. Your success will depend on avoiding distractions.

1. Understand Why Serious Focusing Is Essential

You've had this happen to you: You read for a short time and all of a sudden realize that your brain has been on auto-pilot. You basically forgot what you read. Even if you recalled a little of it, without a high level of concentration you missed some important material and had a low understanding of what you did recall.

When you're *not* focusing strongly, you'll be doing "pseudo work." The author of that term has a useful formula: ***Work Accomplished = Time Spent x Intensity of Focus***.[44] When your intensity is low, you accomplish less. Thus, focusing intensely is critically important and also time-saving. You want to learn as much as you can from each hour of studying, and this chapter provides some key ways to do that.

> The successful warrior is the average man
> with laser-like focus.
> ~ Bruce Lee

2. <u>Avoid Distractions</u>

Since distractions are the cause of most of poor focusing, you need to avoid the four fundamental distractors: multitasking, a disturbing environment, worries, and a lack of interest in your study material.

a. Multitasking, or rather attempting to multitask, is a major distractor. When real thinking is involved, multitasking with two or more tasks is impossible. What's happening is *multi-jumping* or task switching—going from one task to another.[45] To demonstrate:

> --Count by 3s going forward—3, 6, 9, 12, 15, 18, etc. then
> --Count backward by 2s from 18 to 0—18, 16, 14, etc.

Not difficult, but each requires thinking. Now, try to do both counts at the same time. No way! You could jump from one to the other but not do both simultaneously.

To do two things at once is to do neither.
~ Publius Syrus (Syrian slave in Ancient Rome)

While studying, you might begin listening to a song or thinking about a text message. You continue reading, but your brain is paying attention to the song or message. When you switch attention back again, you either must re-read what you didn't read well or go on. Thus, you either waste time re-

reading, or you go on without having learned what you needed to understand what's coming up.

Your focus is like a spotlight, illuminating only where it's pointed at the time. As your attention shifts, the light moves from one place to another, but it can only be focused in one place at a time.[46]

Each attention-switching disrupts your learning, and "studies show that a person who is interrupted takes 50 percent longer to accomplish a task. Furthermore, he or she makes up to 50 percent more errors."[47] Partly that's because of what is missed when you switch your mind away from the study material.

Partly, it's also caused by what was missed even after switching back. You may assume that once you bring your attention back, it's then fully on what you're studying. Nope! You'll experience the problem of *residual attention*.

Residual attention refers to the leftover attention we give to a distraction after that distraction has stopped interfering with our ability to focus . . . . The reality we have to grapple with is that it takes us an average of 1-3 minutes to get our attention back into a space where we are receptive to new information and processing it efficiently, absent the distraction.[48]

The difficulties encountered when you jump away from your study material and then refocus are the penalties you'll pay for attempting to multitask with two or more activities that require serious thinking. It won't be fatal as can happen when you think for a few seconds about an incoming text message when you're driving.[49] Yet, switching away from what you're reading or listening to in school can be quite damaging.

Picking up your cell phone may be the #1 extra task that upsets your study focus. *Turn off your phone when you're doing school work.* A 2014 study found that "even just the presence of a mobile phone led to a 20% reduction in attention, concentration, and performance!"[50]

You live in history's most distracting time in which people tend to quickly jump from reading a headline (but not the article), to a text messages, to a social media site, to music, etc.[51] You may do the same, feeling that you're missing something if you're stuck giving your attention to only one thing. But to learn well, you must do all you can to strongly focus exclusively on the study material and not try to multitask.

b. Disturbing environments occur because of where you're located. Whenever that happens, try to find a quieter place to study.

Avoid studying at a kitchen table with the TV  blaring and people talking. Maybe you could get a table, chair, and lamp in a second-hand store and squeeze them into a quieter place; or find a non-home study location, using a container for school supplies; or get noise-reduction earmuffs or earplugs. If possible, don't study in a noisy area. (Oh, and study on a desk or table if you can. Your brain associates a couch or bed with relaxing and sleeping.[52])

If you want music while studying, make it low-volume and instrumental unless you're doing activities that don't require a strong focus.[53] Better yet, have no music. If you focus at all on the music, it will be distracting.[54]

You may *think* listening to music helps you study more efficiently, but what it actually does is help pass the time, making it seem like you've studied quickly when you've actually been sitting there longer than you should have because you're being lulled by the tunes.[55]

Distractions can occur also because of your location in classes. The back-of-the-room crowd can be disruptive, and sitting in the back means having students, windows, signs on the walls, and other distractions in front of you. "Our visual sense is so dominant that when our eyes are open, much of our attention is distributed immediately to what we see." [56] To hear better and reduce what's between you and the teacher, sit near the front. And, yes, the teacher will then be able to see if you're not focused, but if you want to be a serious learner, that's good.[57]

c. Worrying can be a major distractor.[58] If you think you can resolve a worrisome issue fairly quickly, you can stop studying and do so. If there's no quick solution, then writing down the problem might enable you to put it out of your mind and deal with it later in non-study time. Do whatever you can to prevent any personal concern from interfering with your studying.

d. Lack of interest leads to you going through the motions of studying like a robot without really absorbing much. Even if you eliminate most distractions and focus hard, you may end up with only a hazy idea of what you read. Why? Because you were reading to complete the assignment without caring about the material. *To be effective, you must have an interest in what you're studying.* In that way, you'll be motivated to understand it, and remembering will be easier.[59]

Without interest, you just look at pieces of information with little deep thinking. You learn superficially and forget quickly.

> **Study without desire spoils the memory,**
> **and it retains nothing that it takes in.**
> ~ Leonardo da Vinci

As mentioned in chapter 1, continually seeking personal value and coming up with questions by pre-reading and thinking about your study material is a good way to maintain interest. Have study goals in mind. "Shift all your energy, attention, and focus to what you want to learn."[60]

Since not all distractions can be eliminated, you must learn to concentrate as best you can in spite of them. If you've developed a genuine interest in your studies, you'll be better able to focus fairly well despite minor disturbances.

Note also that even if you initially have little interest, "oftentimes simply 'staying with it' and trying to make it an active part of your thinking will help you develop an interest in that subject."[61]

3. Reduce Your Focusing at Times

It's useful to take both short and long breaks from your intensely focused studying.

a. Short breaks are very useful. It's best to limit your laser-focused study bursts to 20-60 minutes, depending on what you're doing.[62] Then take short breaks to recharge and give your brain a little time to further link new information to prior knowledge.[63]

Don't use breaks to check email, messages, or social networks. That would fill your mind with distracting thoughts. You'll return to your studies "just as frazzled as before the pause, and maybe more so."[64] Your friends can wait for a few hours for you to respond to messages or calls. Get them used to not expecting immediate responses. During breaks, let your mind wander, not seriously thinking about anything. That gives your brain time to process information, move it into long-term memory, and prepare it for new information.[65]

Taking these breaks is also beneficial because your attention weakens after studying for a while, and then you aren't studying effectively. In addition, it's good to get up and move around because prolonged sitting is bad for your health.[66]

Think beforehand, though, about how long your break will be so that a brief break doesn't result in an hour watching TV.[67]

b. Longer-term breaks. These also can be beneficial because they can help you get out of  thinking ruts caused by overfocusing. To explain why, let's look at an analogy (a comparison between two otherwise dissimilar things). Say that you're hungry and searching the refrigerator for something to eat. If you *don't know* what you're looking for, you won't be focused on anything in particular. You're just thinking, "What might be good?." You look around at everything. But what if you *do know* what you're looking for? You're sure it's in a container with a red top. So, you turn on your laser focus to find a container with a red top? You fail to find it because your sister had eaten part of that food and put what was left in a smaller container with a green top. Probably you would have found it if you had not been so intently focused on locating the red top.

This failed refrigerator search is typical of what happens when you get an idea in your head that blinds you to other alternatives. [68] Although it might not be a big deal if you don't find that food, it's a bigger deal if you encounter a math problem you can't solve or a science process you can't figure out because you're intensely focused on an incorrect approach.

Think of your mind as a bowl of ice cream. Imagine pouring hot water from a spoon on the ice cream and then slightly tipping it so that it runs off. After repetitions of this process, the surface of the ice cream would be full of ruts. When information enters the mind, it flows, like water, into the preformed ruts.[69]

When you encounter a problem, you look for stored knowledge in your brain that you may have used previously to help you deal with a similar issue. You usually go down the same brain pathways (of linked brain cells). That's useful if the stored knowledge at the end of the pathways is what you need. When it isn't, a pathway can become a rut you keep going down while ignoring or failing to create other pathways leading to better solutions. "Sometimes, the harder you concentrate, the more you get stuck in those ruts. You can't solve the problem because you fail to see alternative ways of thinking."[70]

The path of least resistance and least trouble is a mental rut already made. It requires troublesome work to undertake the alteration of old beliefs.
~ John Dewey (American philosopher and educational reformer)

In a high-focus mode, you don't want to waste time thinking about things that aren't directly related to the issue at hand.[71] But being convinced that you are right can keep you in a rut.[72]

Sometimes, therefore, you can benefit from getting away from your study material—not focusing or at least going into a lower-focus mode.[73] When you begin studying again, you might have a fresh approach that gets you out of the rut.[74]

Also, even when you aren't focusing, your brain might keep working after you leave your studying. An example is forgetting where you put your keys and unsuccessfully focusing on where you might have put them. Later, when you weren't even thinking about the lost keys, their location pops into your head. Your brain continued to search and found the answer. This occurs when you're awake and often when you're asleep.[75] You can think in terms of having a subconscious mind that sometimes works for you 24/7.[76]

Thus, an advantage of scheduling, to be discussed in the next chapter, is to avoid being caught studying at the last minute, with few or no opportunities for low-focus or no-focus time.

THE BIG PICTURE for Ch. 7

To maximize what I get out of my study time, I should stay highly focused. That means:
--not attempting to multitask,
--minimizing background noises,
--putting worries out of my mind, and
--having interest in what I'm studying.

At times, though, I need to get out of high-focus mode to take short breaks to recharge and think about what I studied. In addition, I can benefit by sometimes leaving my study material for hours or days to get out of thinking ruts and be able to then view the material from a different, more useful perspective.

CHAPTER 8
GET ORGANIZED

Your new learning skills won't help if you misplace assignments or fail to schedule enough study time. Getting organized is not hard, but it requires some thinking and effort.

1. <u>Organize Your Study Material</u>

Organizing is what you do before you do something, so that when you do it, it's not all mixed up.
~ A.A. Milne (author of Winnie the Pooh)

Develop methods for organizing school papers. Instead of a backpack full of binders and papers, use a single 2-inch binder with dividers to separate papers for different classes. To avoid binder overload, occasionally take papers out and put them into folders—organized by subject—in a file cabinet, drawer, or box.[77] In addition, have a plastic pouch or a folder for assignments, as well as a paper or a planner where you can record due dates as soon as you have them. If you just stuff such information into your binder or books, you'll often lose or overlook them.

Create/maintain a system for computer folders and files. Rather than just unsystematically naming documents as you go along, begin each one with a subject and add a title to indicate the contents (e.g., English--term paper). To avoid painful losses, have two copies, one on your computer and another on a cloud account or flash drive. Also, to be able to quickly find your document, put its title somewhere on the first page of your paper.

2. Develop and Maintain Study Schedules

To help manage your time, keep a written study schedule that includes due dates for assignments and exams.

- *Make a complete, updatable master list of what you need to do.*

- *Put tasks from that master list into weekly schedules.*

The master list could have three sub-lists: one for short-term assignments, one for long-term assignments, and one for exams.[78] Then use that master list each weekend to prepare a weekly to-do schedule.

Keep in mind that there will be disruptions, and your work will not always go smoothly. So don't be overly optimistic when deciding the time that will be needed for each task.[79] Add in a little time to account for things not going perfectly.

MASTER SCHEDULE

Short-Term Assignments	Due Date	Comments
~~Social studies, ch. 12~~	~~09/25~~	
~~Spanish, pp. 62-73~~	~~09/26~~	~~Do vocab. cards~~
~~Science, ch. 2~~	~~10/03~~	
Algebra: chs. 4-5	10/07	Talk to Briana on this
History ch. 2	10/08	
Spanish pp. 74-79	10/09	Do vocab. cards
LONG-TERM ASSIGNMENTS	**Due Date**	**Comments**
English term paper ~~Choose Topic~~	~~09/23~~	
~~Do Preliminary. research/outline~~	~~10/04~~	
Do basic research	11/08	Spend Sat. in library
1st draft	11/21	
Final draft	11/30	
Submit paper	12/10	
Science project ~~Choose subject~~	~~10/01~~	
Do research	10/10	Do online research 1st
Get materials	10/14	
Do final research	10/28	
Finish basic project	11/14	
Submit project	11/18	
EXAMS/TESTS	**Due Date**	**Comments**
~~English—test on novel~~	09/27	
~~Spanish—pp. 36-52~~	~~10/14~~	~~Review flash cards~~
Algebra—text chapters 4-5.	10/21	
History—text ch. 20 + handout	10/25	

When putting assignments on your weekly schedule, cross out the corresponding tasks on your master list (as is done above). When you don't finish a task planned for one day on your weekly schedule, transfer it to another day.

If you lack time for the above schedule, *at least*, have a calendar with due dates for exams and major projects.

Weekly Schedule (Oct. 6-12)

TUESDAY	WEDNESDAY
--Dentist appt. 3;45	--Volleyball 3-4:30
--Algebra text pp. 22-33	--Spanish pp. 74-80
--History ch. 2	--Engl. lit bk. ch. 3
--Social Studies ch. 14	--Science text pp. 56-78 quiz
--Work on English term paper due 7/2	--Review Social Studies chs. 6-9

Scheduling keeps you on track, prioritizes your work, and breaks it into reasonably sized portions.

3. Schedule Time for a "Spaced Repetition" Review.

Even when you get a good grasp of your study material, your memory can start to fade rather quickly. Doing a spaced repetition review sometime in the interim period between the end of your studying and your last-minute, pre-exam review can be very beneficial. That review both refreshes your memory and helps ensure that you understand the material as well as you thought you did.

Research has shown that when your brain first puts an item of information into [your] memory, you need to revisit it a few times to increase the chances you'll later be able to find it when you need it. It takes time to move information from working memory to long-term memory. To help with this process, use a technique called *spaced repetition.* This technique involves repeating what you are trying to retain, like a new vocabulary word or a new problem-solving technique, but spacing this repetition over a number of days.[80]

One psychologist's research showed "that people needed to engage with an idea at least three times before they actually learned it."[81] And the U.S. military agrees. They instruct their trainers to present what needs to be learned in three ways: tell them what you're going to tell them, tell them, and tell them what you told them. And the learning that comes from such repetition works even better if the repetitions are spread out over a time period.

Recalling something you learned just minutes or hours ago is of little value. It's fresh in your mind and easy to retrieve. You confidently think you've got it.[82] Oh yeah, sure! What if you wait days or weeks to think about it again, during which you throw many other thoughts into your brain? Then, can you find that memory, or have you partially or totally forgotten it?

When you do spaced repetition, you must make serious efforts to remember what you forgot after each space away from your study material. The struggle to remember gets that material more firmly into your brain and makes it easier to recall later.[83]

Spaced repetition can be made more effective if you combine it with what's called *retrieval practice*. This means you try to recall what you studied and partially forgot without first looking at your book or notes. That's a true test of whether you really know and remember it. This way of checking your knowledge is what is meant by retrieval practice—"drawing ideas you're starting to learn from your own mind rather than simply looking at the answer." [84] There's not much struggling and learning value if all you do is to read your bracketed passages or your notes. [85] Such reviewing may give you the *impression* that you know the material well.[86] I read it before; I just read it again; I understand and can remember it." It's likely, however, that it will fade away rather rapidly.

By doing retrieval practice after a time away from your studying, you'll avoid the impression you know it all. More likely reactions will be: "Oh, I forgot that part" or "I didn't get that quite right." By working to get it right, the information will be better understood and more likely to stick in your mind.

Doing spaced repetition/retrieval practice is quite different from cramming; that is, bunching all your studying of your material into one period. Cramming doesn't give you enough time to consolidate the information in your mind. You may believe you really know the material, but you probably fail to put it solidly into your memory.

> Research about cramming shows that as little as a day or two following a cram session, you will no longer remember much. Within a week, you will likely have forgotten 75% or more of the material you studied. [87]

Therefore, avoid the need to cram. Try to arrange your schedule so that you have the time to do spaced repetition and retrieval practice.

4. Summary

Knowing what you must do is well worth the time spent on scheduling. Instead of thinking about when to study, you look at your schedule and say, "Yeah, I need to do that part of my study schedule."[88] You get it done.[89]

> Organization is the single most important factor in creating useful intelligence, and it is a *learned* skill. By consciously becoming more organized, you really increase your learning effectiveness.[90]

THE BIG PICTURE for Ch, 8

Minutes spent on organizing my school materials and maintaining study schedules will save hours later, avoid mistakes, and provide time to think about what I'm learning. I need to determine the best ways to do those things and consistently practice them.

An important benefit I can gain from organizing is to have sufficient time to do spaced repetition (using retrieval practice) sometime between finishing the four strategy steps and the exam. That will increase my understanding and memory.

CHAPTER 9
BE ABLE TO REMEMBER BETTER

Learning goes way beyond memorizing.

At the end of the day, though, you need to do more than make an excellent set of notes—you need to find ways of getting the key information into your memory in a form that can be used for practical situations.[91]

1. Appreciate Importance of Memory Skills

Remembering is difficult. You can read a whole book and soon forget almost all of it—as related by a highly educated reporter and author:

Looking up at my shelves, at books that have drained so many of my waking hours is always a dispiriting experience. *One Hundred Years of Solitude*: I remember magical realism and that I enjoyed it. But that's about it. I don't even recall when I read it. About *Wuthering Heights* I remember exactly two things: that I read it in high school and there was a character named Heathcliff. I couldn't say whether I liked the book or not.[92]

That this highly educated reporter, who later became a memory-competition champion, would have such memory issues shows that you just can't read along and expect the information to go into your brain in ways you can remember well.

Some say that's not important—that, instead, you should be learning to reason, analyze, problem-solve, etc. A few even say you can always look up what you need. Without enough remembered knowledge, though, you often won't know what to search for. Furthermore, the "answer" to your search can be just an isolated piece of information unless you have other knowledge to make it understandable. [93] Then too, when you analyze, evaluate, etc., you connect to prior knowledge.[94] "The process of reasoning requires us to shift through our rich store of memories, using tools that have proven useful in the past to make informed and productive decisions."[95]

Thus, developing effective memory skills is extremely useful. To do that, it helps to understand how memory operates.

2. <u>Know How Memory Works</u>

As stated by an eight-time World Memory Champion: "Association is at the heart of developing a perfect memory. It is the mechanism by which memory works."[96] In fact, according to an International Grand Master of Memory: "We learn only by association. It doesn't happen in any other way."[97]

You associate (connect, link, relate) what you want to remember to other information that's in your brain. That could be information that's been in your long-term memory for years, or something you just added to your memory.

An example of the latter would be trying to remember the Spanish word for dessert—*postre* (pronounced pos-tray). You form a visual image that's easy to recall, such as a post with a tray on

top filled with desserts. [98] That linked image then in your memory is easier to recall than the vocabulary word, and recalling the picture can remind you of the word *postre*.

We frequently experience retrieval (pulling from memory) problems. "I know that; I just can't quite remember it. It's on the tip of my tongue. Could you give me a clue?" You'd love to have a clue—some hint to help you recall a memory.[99]

If, when storing a memory, you do so with a clue or *hook* to pull it out, you'll have a clear, direct connection between the hook and what you want to recall.[100]

One brain scientist thinks in terms of handles. "The more handles one creates at the moment of learning, the more likely the information can be accessed at a later date."[101] Hook, hint, link, clue, handle—the principle is the same. "Any information that has been associated with what you have learned can potentially serve as cues to later access the information from your memory."[102]

As one learning expert explains:

If you're having trouble remembering something, it's because you aren't presenting it to your brain in a way it can handle it efficiently. The trick is to find a way to hook that information to things your brain can store and recall easily. In a way, the hard-to-remember information piggybacks on the easy-to-remember information.[103]

For example, say you want to remember the five Great Lakes—Huron, Ontario, Michigan, Erie, and Superior. You can try to do that by repeating the names over and over: Huron, Huron, Ontario, Ontario, etc. That process, though, might turn off your brain. After hearing Huron, Huron, Huron, your brain says, "Huron, yeah, I know that; I'm no longer paying attention."[104] Or you may simply become bored and quit.

A better remembering technique would be to use the hook-word HOMES, which consists of the first letters of the Great Lakes: **H**uron, **O**ntario, **M**ichigan, **E**rie, and **S**uperior. Take a minute to review the connection between the HOMES and the lakes. You'll be impressed that weeks, months, even years later, when you try to remember the lakes, HOMES will come to mind as a good way to do that.

While you're aware of the association involved with the *postre* picture and the HOMES acronym (that is, an abbreviation formed from the first letters of other words), you're often not consciously aware of any connection. For example, you're in Room A thinking about something you need to do in Room B. In Room B you forget what you wanted to do. Going back to Room A might revive your memory because Room A was *associated* with making your original memory. That shows how recalling one memory (of being in Room A) can help you recall a related memory (what you wanted to do in Room B), even if you didn't realize that you made such an association.

You can make both conscious and unconscious associations between new information and other memories. You also can make mixtures of the two. For example, let's say you *consciously* made the HOMES hook, but you also previously read a book with a story that took place in Chicago and made references to nearby Lake Michigan. You weren't trying to remember that lake, but it was mentioned several times; it pretty much *unconsciously* stayed in your memory, and made it easier to recall that it's one of the five Great Lakes.

Even though such mixed associations exist, for explanatory purposes, we'll look only at hook-making as being done consciously or unconsciously.

Since most of the examples so far have been of conscious associations, we'll now look at unconscious linkages. Then we'll get back with some more detailed information on making conscious associations—the ones you have more control over.

3. <u>Make Unconscious Associations</u>

Most consciously created hooking is done to help in remembering simple, concrete things, such as the five Great Lakes or a vocabulary word. Others are slightly more complicated, but still deal with fairly simple information. What, though, about remembering the nature of a novel, or of a lengthy mathematical or scientific process, or of the theme and events in a history chapter? You can consciously make hooks to remember some of the details, but not easily for larger interrelated, complicated information. For bigger subjects, associations are mostly made unconsciously among the various memory pieces as you study.

The main way you can improve how well you remember something in an unconscious or semi-conscious way is to fully *understand* the study material.

In the process of fully understanding new information, you make many unconscious connections in your brain. For example, understanding a novel involves linking together knowledge of the characters, the plot, and other story elements, as well as linking those elements to pieces of previous knowledge of what you knew about similar characters, stories, etc. You might be aware of making some of these linkages, but others were essentially done unconsciously. Understanding creates a memory network of these links; that is, of mental associations that can serve to recall the new information.[105] The more you gain an understanding, the more you'll be able to use the study material in the future and be much less likely to forget it.[106]

4. More on Making Conscious Associations

The techniques described below are only a small sample of possible ways to remember by using different types of consciously developed hooks to help you remember other pieces of information. Before you resort to using standard techniques, however, first try to create original hooks that are personally meaningful to you. Those will usually stick with you better.[107]

For example, suppose you want to remember the medicine *gabapentin*. You can picture a guy talking away (<u>gab</u>bing) while using a <u>pen</u> to poke a <u>tin</u> can. Or you could create some other hook for remembering gabapentin that might borrow from other techniques described below. That's why they're provided: to be used in standard ways and to suggest ideas for you on how to make more original, personally meaningful hooks.

To learn about more memory techniques and develop a super memory, you could study a memory book over the summer. That might enable you to thereafter amaze your friends, do better at school, and acquire a life-long skill. Good books include *Unlimited Memory* by Kevin Horsley, *Memory Super-Powers!* by Nelson Dellis, and *The Memory Book* by Harry Loyrane and Jerry Lucas.

The following memory techniques came from these and other memory books. They should give you good ideas you can use for remembering things. You don't have to be a memory master like the authors of the above books to be able to use such techniques, even though reading one of those books would advance your remembering skills substantially.

SAMPLES OF HOOKING TECHNIQUES

You already saw one standard technique: Create an ACRONYM to serve as a hook. Again, an acronym—such as HOMES—is made up of the first letters of what you want to remember, in this case the five lakes (Huron, Ontario, Michigan, Erie, and Superior).

For the order for doing mathematical operations (Parentheses, Exponents, Multiply, Divide, Add, Subtract), you can use an **ACROSTIC**—lines of words or sentences with letters, usually the first ones, to indicate what you want to remember. One would be **P**lease **E**xcuse **M**y **D**ear **A**unt **S**ally.[108] Remember that, and you'll know when to do each operation.

Hard-to-Recall Info.	Easier-to-Recall Hook
Parentheses, Exponents, Multiply, Divide, Add, Subtract	**P**lease **E**xcuse **M**y **D**ear **A**unt **S**ally

How about remembering formulas? Ugh! How do you do that other than by repeating them over and over? One way is to use **STORIES**. Here's a tiny story for remembering the formula for the area of a triangle.

The Formula   *The Story Hook*

"Triangle area = ½ bh

b=base; h=height

Walk <u>half</u>way (1/2) up a triangle. Realize you must get down. Jump on its <u>base</u>. Then jump as <u>high</u> as you can."[109]

Here's another story for remembering the more complicated quadratic formula.

$$x = \frac{-b \pm \sqrt{b^2 - 4ac}}{2a}$$

There was a "negative boy who couldn't decide, yes or no, to go to a radical party. But the boy was a square and he missed out on four awesome chicks. And the party was all over at 2 a.m."[110] Thus, you remember by recalling the story of a negative boy (**-b**), yes or no (**±**), radical party ($\sqrt{}$), square boy (**b²**), -4 awesome chicks (**-4ac**), 2 a.m. (**2a**).

Hard-to-Recall Info.	Easier-to-Recall Hook
Quadratic Formula	Story

You also use **IMAGES**, such as the previously mentioned desserts on a tray on a post to remember the Spanish word (*postre*) for dessert. In general, we're good at remembering visual images, but "terrible at remembering other kinds of information, like lists of words or numbers."[111] In fact, "the 'big secret'

74

behind tripling your memory boils down to imagining pictures in our head."[112] *A hook that can be visualized is usually the best*, with pictures that are unusual or have emotion tied to them being the very best.[113]

Hooking can use more than one technique. IMAGE + STORY is a common combination,[114] such as with the triangle above (with base and height), along with the story of jumping up and down. And here's where you can become very creative in developing a hook. *Any* story, or *any* combination can be used as a hook if it's meaningful to you.

Another category of memory techniques is the use of PRE-MEMORIZED SYSTEMS. The 2,500-years-old Memory Palace Method (also called the Journey Method or Method of Loci [pronounced *low-sigh*]) is one such system.[115] It's a two-step method that relies on memorized images.[116]

1. Memorize several places. These could be places in your home (e.g., the kitchen sink, your bed, a shower) or places in your town (a gas station, library, drug store), or anywhere. You can even use your body parts.

2. Connect the locations with what you want to remember, such as a 12-item grocery shopping list. You imagine a bananas in your *kitchen sink*, mac and cheese spread on your *bed*, carrots coming out of your *shower*, and nine

more items connected to pre-memorized locations in your home. In the grocery store, one by one you recall your list of 12 locations as you mentally walk through the previously memorized places in your home. The grocery items come to mind: kitchen sink—bananas, etc. (Search online for "Memory Palace" or "Loci System" and you'll find good videos about this method.)

Hard-to-Recall Info.	Easier-to-Recall Hook
12 Grocery Items 1)	12 Pre-Memorized Places Linked to the 12 Grocery Items

A second example of a pre-memorized method is the rhyme system for remembering numbers.[117] It goes like this:

0 = Hero	5 = Hive
1 = Bun	6 = Sticks
2 = Shoe	7 = Heaven
3 = Tree	8 = Gate
4 = Door	9 = Vine

Ulysses, a 730-page novel by the Irish writer James Joyce, was about events that took place in a single day: 6/16/1904. How to remember that date? A stick (6) went into a bun (1). Another stick (6) went into another bun (1). A vine (9) grew around the sticks, but a hero (0) pulled the vine away and then walked away through a doorway (4). You can use other words as long as they rhyme with the numbers.

Hard-to-Recall Info.	Easier-to-Recall Hook
day/month/year	7 rhymed words making up a story

THE BIG PICTURE for Ch. 9

I can relate new information to pre-existing memories or to memory hooks I just created. The associations that are made help me later when I'm trying to recall the new information. That's because a relatively easy-to-remember piece of linked information in my memory can serve as a reminder of the new, harder-to-remember information.

These connections can be made consciously or unconsciously. With unconsciously associated connections, the better I understand that new info., the more such linkages will be made to other info. in my brain, and the better I'll be able to remember.

PART 3
HAVE A PRODUCTIVE
ATTITUDE

CHAPTER 10
ADOPT A GROWTH MINDSET

How much you think you can improve will affect how much you do improve. While you now have a good learning strategy, you still might wonder if you can really be a successful learner. You may think you're just an average or below-average student forever—or maybe no student at all, just waiting for school to end. You see others getting higher grades, apparently with less effort, and you assume that school is not where you're going to excel. If that's what you believe, you'll find it difficult to succeed. You may have this elephant's attitude:

> Think of a young elephant tied to a stake in the ground. When it's a baby, the elephant isn't strong enough to pull the stake up, so it eventually stops trying because it learns that the effort is futile. As the elephant grows, it gains more than enough power and strength to pull out the stake, but it remains tied up by something as small as a rope and a flimsy piece of metal because of what it learned as a baby. In psychology, it's called learned helplessness.

> Most of us behave like that elephant. At some point, we had an experience that gave us the impression of what we're capable of, and our belief about a low potential has been set ever since. But just as helplessness is learned, it's as just possible to learn to be limitless.[118]

To realize your potential, the key is to **change from a FIXED mindset to a GROWTH mindset.** *That is, change from thinking you have a fixed (unchangeable) level of intelligence—to understanding that your mental qualities can be improved (grow) through your efforts.*[119]

With a fixed mindset you believe people are either smart or not, or school-smart or not. If you're smart, you don't have to work hard to do well. Therefore, if you need to work hard, that means you're not smart. Sounds logical, but these are erroneous beliefs that will prevent you from improving.[120]

You absolutely can go beyond your current ability level, and doing so is largely within your own control.[121] Parts of your brain can reorganize and even grow. [122] Musicians and other specialists continually experience this. [123] An extreme example was the sizable growth of a part of the brains of taxi drivers in London, England who studied years for a test on knowing about 25,000 city streets.[124] Your brain is adaptable.[125]

> [It's] like a muscle—it gets stronger when you use it. And scientists have been able to show just how the brain grows and gets stronger when you learn. Tiny connections in the brain actually multiply and get stronger. The more you challenge your mind to learn, the more

your brain cells grow. Then, things that you once found very hard or even impossible—like speaking a foreign language or doing algebra—seem to become easy. The result is a stronger, smarter brain.[126]

Realizing how your abilities can grow is critical for your success.[127] As Henry Ford said: "Whether you believe you can do a thing or not, you are right."[128] But that's not to say that making a large, improve-your-abilities effort will be easy!

One obstacle to adopting a growth mindset is that you like to do what you do well, not what you do poorly.[129] You can feel bad if you must *at first* work harder than others to get the same or even lower grades. You might prefer to get a D and tell others (and yourself) that you did poorly because you didn't study much, rather than get a C after hard studying. You'd rather be "perceived as lazy than stupid."[130] So you don't do the work you need to improve.

Another obstacle might arise if you're not from the dominant culture. Because of that you may feel bad at times. Your life experiences have been somewhat different from those of many of your teachers and textbook authors. Thus, there will be times when you don't quickly see where they're coming from. Likewise, your teachers sometimes can fail to understand how you're interpreting things.[131]

While that can create awkward moments, such differences also can be advantages. If, when you're young, you knew two languages, or spoke standard and non-standard English, you know that there're two ways to say the same thing. That helps you develop a more flexible mind.[132] Also, thinking a little differently from the majority can make you more creative. Moreover, looking at the dominant culture from the outside makes you more observant and sensitive. Profit from those advantages and learn from any difficulties you encounter.

A third obstacle comes forth if you fear and react quite negatively to failures. You need to realize that whenever you're challenging yourself, you'll fail at times.[133] Only if you're doing the easiest things can you avoid mistakes.[134] Expect some failures and bounce back.[135] Making mistakes is part of the improvement process. It's a terrible waste not to learn from what caused your mistakes. Thomas Edison had the right attitude. As this inventor of the light bulb famously said: "I have not failed. I've just found 10,000 ways that won't work." So he learned and tried other ways until he succeeded.

When we fail, "we search for meaning, and so we learn more effectively. Errors create meaning. They build understanding."[136]

I've missed more than 9,000 shots in my career.
I've lost almost 300 games. 26 times, I've been
trusted to take the game-winning shot and missed.
I've failed over and over again in my life.
And that's why I succeed.
~ Michael Jordan[137]

You might think: "If I were as good as Michael Jorden, I wouldn't mind admitting to missing some shots." The point, though, is that he became a super star by learning from his mistakes. He wasn't always great. He was cut from his high school varsity team—which motivated him to intensely practicing until he made it back on. He didn't get an offer from the college he wanted—but his eventual "college coach was taken aback by his willingness to work harder than anyone else."[138] He rose to the top by hard work and learning from his mistakes.

The difference between average people and
achieving people is their perception of
and response to failure.
~ John C. Maxwell (author focusing on leadership)

Your success depends more on your attitude and study strategy than on your current ability level.[139] Whatever your starting level, you can be an achiever with the right attitude and an effective study strategy. You're not stuck where you are if you're willing to put in the effort needed to improve and to use effective study methods. If you do that, you're the smart one, and eventually you won't have to work as hard.

THE BIG PICTURE for Ch. 10

I'm pretty sure that most people believe that the brain you were given is the brain you'll have forever—that some students are simply good at school stuff, and some aren't. With hard work, though, scientists have shown the brain can get stronger just like an exercised muscle gets stronger. It may take time, but I can now see how having a growth mindset, along with a good learning strategy and a determination to study seriously, can bring success.

CHAPTER 11
KEEP AT IT; DON'T GET DISCOURAGED

Even when you combine hard work with a good learning strategy and a belief that you can improve, your progress can be slowed by a lack of accumulated knowledge and/or getting into unproductive moods.

1. <u>Understand the Need to Build Background Knowledge</u>

As explained earlier: "Our brains 'bundle' new information with previous information, using the old knowledge to help us make meaning out of the new knowledge." [140] The more prior knowledge you have, the easier it is to understand something new. The more we learn and retain, the more we can learn and retain." [141] The more you know about the French Revolution, the easier it will be to understand the Russian Revolution. [142]

We continually acquire knowledge—not only facts, but also ways to analyze, evaluate, use our imagination, and apply other skills.

> Much of the time when we see someone apparently engaged in logical thinking, he or she is actually engaged in memory retrieval. When faced with a problem, you first search for a solution in memory. [143]

You look for previously learned information and processes you can use. "The more knowledge held in long-term memory, the easier it is to add more."[144]

All New Learning Builds on Previous Learning

Let's say you thoroughly studied an article on diabetes, but some other students did better on the exam because they knew more about diabetes or diseases in general before they read the assignment. They just had to learn some of the new material. You had to learn all of the new information. They also could more quickly get a fuller understanding of the article and more easily remember its contents because their ability to link it to their previous knowledge that made it more meaningful.[145]

If you've lacked opportunities for acquiring good background knowledge, you can *Catch Up or Give Up.*[146] To catch up, to increase your knowledge, you need to:

- Work hard to think about and remember more of what's in your regular school work,

- Constantly look up unknowns, and

- Do outside reading, especially in the summer.

Through reading, I escaped the bad parts of my life in the South Bronx. And, through books, I got to travel the world and the universe. To me it was a passport out of my childhood, and it remains a way – through the power of words - to change the world.
~ Sonia Sotomayor—Supreme Court Justice

Thus, if your lack of background knowledge causes difficulties, keep doing your best while working to increase that knowledge.

Do the best you can until you know better.
Then when you know better, do better.
~ Maya Angelou (Poet, author, & civil rights activist)

2. Understand That Some Boring Material Is Critical

"This course is b-o-r-i-n-g. I really can't get into it." Imagine that you have a thick chemistry or biology textbook that has page after page of facts and concepts you have to learn and remember. That looks pretty dull and will require hard work. Yet, to do advanced work in those fields and most others, you have to first learn the fundamentals— to master what's in those books. It's like learning to play basketball. Initially, you need to practice dribbling and shooting lay-ups, learn the rules of the game, etc. before you're ready to play well. Yes, that's more pleasant than learning all the fundamental information in those textbooks. But that textbook learning eventually can lead to more interesting advanced courses and a fulfilling, well-paid career. That's something to keep in mind if you're not likely to be drafted by an NBA team.

In addition to placing a high value on that basic information, a good way to overcome the boredom factor is to take on the learning process as a challenge. You can make it a personal quest to apply all you've learned in this book to do well, To the extent you succeed you also build up useful accumulated knowledge in your brain.

3. Overcome Unproductive Moods

"I don't understand what I'm reading," "I'm never going to learn this." "I should be able to get this faster." "Why do I keep making mistakes?" Such negative thoughts and moods that come with them will distract you, maybe even make you give up.[147]

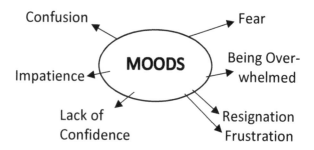

Everyone becomes frustrated at times. When this happens, a good option is to back away from what you're studying for a while. Coming back with a fresh perspective could solve your problem and cancel the bad mood.[148]

Another approach whenever you have such emotional feelings is to stop, analyze what's upsetting you, and fight to come out of it.

> Once you identify the voices in your head that are telling you what you can't do, start talking back to them. When you find yourself thinking, "I always screw up on this sort of thing," counter with, "Just because I haven't always been good at this in the past doesn't mean that I can't be great at it now."[149]

Fully acknowledge your negative emotions and try to overcome them.[150] If you think you're terrible at math, ask yourself if that's surely true, or if maybe you just need to change how you study math.[151]

Just do the best you can. No one can do better than that.

~ John Wooden   (Basketball coach and author)

THE BIG PICTURE for Ch. 11

Even if I do everything right, a lack of background knowledge can reduce my ability to absorb new information and do well on exams. I need to keep working to build up that knowledge base. Furthermore, as I proceed to learn more, I need to fight off frustrations and bad moods I encounter along the way and just do the best I can.

CHAPTER 12
BE CAREFUL AND CALM ON EXAM DAY

While what you learn is more important than your grades, little progress with grades can be discouraging. If you're using good study methods and working hard, but still testing poorly, you might simply need more time to build your background knowledge. On the other hand, it could be that you're making unnecessary exam mistakes. Below are a few tips to help you read test questions, manage your exam time, and reduce nervousness.

Keep in mind this British World War II poster used when London was being bombed day and night—Keep calm and carry on. *Don't rush to answer the questions*.

1. Scan the exam, get an idea of the questions, and decide how to use your time to answer them.[152]

2. Carefully read instructions and wording of the questions.

3. Don't panic if you think you'll have trouble with any questions.[153]

Even with multiple-choice or true-false questions, a careful reading the wording of questions can be critical. Wrong answers often have some partially correct information that causes you, without careful reading, to choose the wrong option. With essay questions, note whether the teacher is asking to describe, evaluate, apply a basic principle, or whatever.[154] Read each word and underline the ones that tell you what to do.[155] And take a good look at the whole test. If you're rushing, you could make serious errors, like failing to notice there are questions on the back of a sheet.

Also, be sure that you're answering the question, not what you think is being asked. For example, when making study notes, you tend to think about the material in a certain way that might not be exactly what the question is all about. Don't rush and give a wonderful answer to the wrong question.[156]

With essay questions, in the test paper's margin, make a quick outline of the major points to include in your answer. That will help you write a well-organized essay. Also, especially with STEM questions, "jot down any thoughts that come to mind, such as specific formulas or possible approaches for solving the problem."[157]

The temptation is to quickly start writing and think of what to say as you go along. That's a recipe for forgetting important points and writing an unimpressive, meandering essay. Having a brief outline or other key notes will save time and produce a superior product. "Don't start writing until you know how the essay will end."[158]

Finally, keeping calm is extremely important. "If we are preoccupied by worries that we're going to flunk the test, we have that much less attention to expend on figuring out the answers."[159] So stop and take some deep breaths.[160] Maybe close your eyes until you can get your concentration back. [161] Before the exam even begins, you can sit still and do some deep breathing. That will be calming, and you won't feel that you're losing exam time by taking that tiny, pre-exam procedure.

The very best way to stay calm? Review your notes using spaced repetition and retrieval practice until you're sure you know the material well. Then walk into your exam "already confident of your stellar performance. No muscles tightening, no anxiety, just a cool, calm, and collected top-rate student reporting for duty."[162]

THE BIG PICTURE for Ch. 12

I can improve my exam performance by:

--Carefully reading the questions,

--Jotting down major points for essay questions,

--Staying calm, and

--Being well prepared.

SUMMARY

When you practice the methods in this book, you'll become much more successful in learning anything in the future. Of course, it's not as simple as 1, 2, 3—or in this case strategy-steps 1, 2, 3, 4. You're going to have to work hard. "The only place *success* comes before *work* is in the dictionary."[163]

Decide what your success goal is. That might be to use your study time more effectively; to prove to yourself and others you can excel academically; to get the grades needed to be accepted into a college or other school, possibly with a scholarship; or to achieve some other objective. Having a clear purpose will bring more energy and better focus when using the learning tools you now have. Then go for it.[164]

You might begin by practicing the strategy steps one at a time; for example by studying with a questioning mind in week one and beginning to effectively identify important information in week two, with the goal of thoroughly understanding each step and then combining them with steps three and four.[165] Or, better yet, you can try to use all four steps from the beginning.

Don't expect to become a straight-A student overnight. You'll need to improve your strategy execution by getting a little better each day until you master the four steps (chapters 2-5) and regularly practice the ways to enhance your strategy execution (chapters 6-8) and improve your attitude and test-taking abilities (chapters 10-12) That's the way learning normally progresses. [166] Stick to it, though, and you'll succeed.

By reading the three appendixes to this book, you'll be able to do even better.

APPENDIXES

APPENDIX A
KNOW A LITTLE ABOUT YOUR BRAIN

APPENDIX B
IMPROVE LIFESTYLE FOR BETTER LEARNING

APPENDIX C
USE ABBREVIATIONS FOR FASTER WRITING

APPENDIX A
KNOW A LITTLE ABOUT YOUR BRAIN

A dictionary definition of **to learn** is "to gain knowledge, comprehension, or mastery of through study or experience."[167] Your brain, however, has a different definition: *"Learning involves making new connections between clusters of neurons in different parts of the brain."*[168] After reading this appendix, if you understand what that means, you'll have grasped the basic way in which your brain functions for learning.

Your learning happens in brain cells called **neurons**. You probably have over 80 billion of them! [169] To the left is what a couple of neurons look like. Notice the **dendrites** and the **axon terminals**. For neurons to communicate, electrically charged

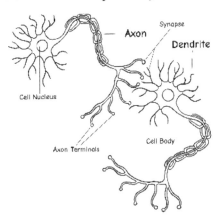

chemical signals are sent over tiny gaps (**synapses**) between the *axons* of one neuron and the *dendrites* of another. [170] If the signal remains strong, the neurons stay linked.

You have networks or webs of neurons with many such connections. These are not like physically connected spider webs. A neuron web is held together by the dendrite ↔ axon signals. If those signals weaken or die, the memory will be harder or impossible to find. If the signals get stronger and/or their numbers increase, you can more easily retrieve your memory.[171]

Knowledge of how these neurons work will help you understand how you remember new information.

UNDERSTANDING

Earlier you learned that you understand new information by relating it with previous knowledge; that is, by associating the new information with memories already in your brain that help you make sense out of the new material.

Those memories are located in webs of neurons spread around your brain, with connections among neurons made with amazing speed.[172] No single neuron contains a full memory. Rather, individual neurons have bits and pieces of information that together make up what you've placed into your memory.[173] Recalling some of these bits can get into the web that has associations with what you're trying to

The shape, color, and smell of an orange, for example, are categorized and stored in different sets of neurons. Activating those sites simultaneously brings together a recollection of our thoughts and experiences involving an orange.[175]

If you have very few neuron webs of previous knowledge to help you understand a particular piece of new information, the related learning will be more difficult than if you had more. As mentioned before, you can more easily understand an article on diabetes if you already knew something about diabetes or diseases in general. The more you learn, the easier it will be to learn more.[176]

REMEMBERING

Most of what you see or hear never gets into a neuron web. And that's good. You don't want remember unessential information. Let's say that you're looking out a bus window. You see buildings, signs, and people. Some of those sights might enter into your brain, but they'll disappear in a few seconds if you don't consider them worth thinking about.

Here's a school-related example. You're doing an algebra homework assignment. The text mentions that the method for solving the problem was developed by Otto von Squat in 1833. Well done

Otto, but that bit of unimportant knowledge quickly fades away. It may enter into your mind, but it only stays there for a few seconds because you didn't believe it was important enough to think about.

It's different when you read about the method for solving the algebra problem. That's important, and you start thinking about it. It enters into what's called **working memory** and sticks around while you're still thinking about it.

Next, you want to move the new information in working memory into one or more long-term memory webs. That's not easy. It can take some time and effort before you can get the new material connected to old information and moved solidly into long-term memory.[177]

Once in a while information can go into long-term memory almost directly—if it has an excellent prior knowledge connection. An illustration would be getting a lock with a combination that matches your birthday's month/day/year. With that wonderful association, the combination can go straight into long-term memory. Normally, though, the process takes much longer.[178]

And there are two big problems with short-term memory.

1. *It's quite short.* As stated previously, you might, in a matter of seconds, forget the new information unless you begin thinking about it.[179]

2. *It has an extremely limited capacity.* Only about three to seven new items that can be held in your short-term memory at one time.[180]

Even seven items can be a stretch. Try remembering this phone number: 301-275-8374. Assume that 301 is your area code that you hardly have to think about. That leaves seven digits. To copy those numbers, most people would look at 275 and copy it, then look at 8374 and copy that. Why not just look at and copy all seven numbers once? Because it's difficult to remember all seven digits, even briefly. The average capacity of immediate memory is less than seven items.[181]

Suppose that you get past these time and capacity limitations and successfully link new information to prior-knowledge neuron webs. You still can't assume that you've jumped over a wall and have safe, solid, long-term memories on the other side. Usually, memories are still fragile when they first arrive from working memory, and they spend some time in one part of the brain (the hippocampus) "while they are maturing, before they are properly stored elsewhere in the brain." [182] "Maturing" means making and strengthening connections with neuron webs.[183]

Furthermore, forgetting occurs if the memory webs are seldom used and the connections fade or disappear. [184] Repetition helps strengthen the signals and increase the number of linkages.[185]

The brief information above provides an extremely basic, oversimplified explanation of how your brain deals with new information. This short description should, nevertheless, help in understanding how the four steps in the learning process relate to your learning, as summarized below

STEP 1: STUDY WITH A QUESTIONING MIND

You experience the limited, short-term memory capacity issue when you're reading. You take in some new study information, and then get distracted by your phone, worries, noise, or whatever. Such distractions can go into your short-term memory and crowd out the study material. Studying with a questioning mind gives you a stronger focus that helps protect you from paying attention to memory-robbing distractions.

STEP 2: IDENTIFY IMPORTANT INFORMATION

The short-term memory capacity problem also affects how quicky you forget what just entered your mind. What you get from reading page 57 can be knocked out of your limited space by new information on page 59, and so on. At the end of an assignment you've then forgotten a lot. That's why you need to mark what you think is important as you go along and go back later to carefully select what then seems to be most important and worth getting into your long-term memory.

STEP 3: GET THE BIG PICTURE

When reading, you initially make only weak connections between pieces of new information with neuro webs of previous knowledge. When developing a big picture, however, you think about how the pieces of the new information fit together and relate to older information. In the process you gain greater understanding and memory by making additional neuron connections, strengthening existing synapses between neurons, and creating a larger web of linked neurons.

STEP 4: MAKE NOTES

The thinking you do while making notes in your own words and way results in even more neuron connections.

APPENDIX B
IMPROVE LIFESTYLE FOR BETTER LEARNING

Even if you've become an effective learner, there are things that reduce your brain power and make learning more difficult. Or, stated more positivly, there are ways in which you can sharpen your brain. What you do in four areas has major effects.

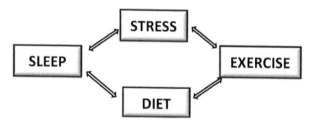

STRESSED BRAINS DON'T WORK WELL

Short-term stress can be useful by releasing hormones that help you react quickly to urgent situations. This type of stress normally lasts for seconds or minutes until you've dealt with the emergency.[186] Alas, the effects are harmful, when your stress continues for long periods.[187]

Long-term (chronic) stress can both devastate your health and reduce your ability to learn.

You can see the effects of stress on learning in everyday life. Stressed people don't do math very well. They don't process language very efficiently. They have poorer memories . . . . Stressed individuals do not generalize or adapt old pieces of information to new scenarios as well as non-stressed individuals. They can't concentrate. In almost every way it can be tested, chronic stress hurts our ability to learn.[188]

 Recall that learning can make the brain grow. Chronic stress has the opposite effect. It hinders the development of the part of the brain that controls your most complex mental functions, and it affects your ability to regulate emotions.[189] It can slow the growth of brain cells and may rewire your brain in harmful ways.[190]

Your brain wasn't made for long-term stress. You want to avoid or at least reduce it. Although a lengthy discussion of how to cope with stress is outside the scope of this book, here are three basic recommendations for dealing with this problem.

1. *Try to identify the source or sources of your stress*, such as difficulties with your family, violence in your neighborhood, or rejection by others. Determine what you might be able to do to improve the situation. This thinking will at least give you a better understanding of your stress and a greater sense of control.

2. *Seek help in dealing with stress.* Being alone with stress can make it worse. Talking with your friends or family could help. But that may not be practical. Indeed, those people might be part of what's stressing you. Or possibly, you can't identify the source of your stress. It might relate to some deeply distressing event that occurred so early in your childhood you don't remember it, or it's so painful that you've mentally blocked out the memory. [191] The best approach then could be to seek professional help, perhaps starting with your school counselor. That would be especially useful if you're having difficulties controlling your emotions, which is a strong indication of the lasting effects of trauma.

3. *Realize how stress harms your ability to focus and try to push it aside as much as possible when studying.* That's easier said than done, but when stressful thoughts are competing for your focus, you won't be able to study effectively. Thus, try as hard as you can when reading or listening in class to tell yourself: "I need to block out all disruptors to what I'm doing right now."

"EXERCISE BOOSTS BRAIN POWER"[192]

Sure, you can be totally out of shape and sit at a desk  or in a classroom chair. But exercise is one of the best things you can do for better learning. When you exercise, specific neurochemicals and proteins in your brain are released in greater amounts and improve your ability to learn and remember.[193]

A key protein created by exercise is brain-derived neurotrophic factor (BDNF). That helps make connections between brain cells, keeps them healthy, and encourages the formation of new cells. [194] Exercise also increases production of neurochemicals that "help your brain to be alert, attentive, motivated for learning, and positive toward learning."[195]

Without going into complicated scientific explanations of how exercise improves learning, understand that it does. It also is one of the best ways to combat stress and depression.

Therefore, do some exercising to pump up your brain as well as your body.[196] "You don't have to be an Olympic athlete to keep your brain sharp. There's ample evidence to show that even 10 minutes of aerobic exercise a day can have enormous benefits."[197] Moderate exercising, such as walking instead of riding in a car, can have meaningful effects.

BRAINS, LIKE CARS, NEED GOOD FUEL

"There's a direct connection between a good diet and a healthy brain."[198] Your brain needs energy from a healthy, balanced diet and adequate water.[199]

Try to avoid "fake foods" that have had most of the nutrition processed out of them. These include french fries, chips, chicken nuggets, and anything with lots of sugar or white flour, like doughnuts, surgery breakfast cereals, and soft drinks. [200] Refined sugar contributes to impaired brain function. leads to inflammation, and can even cause depression."[201]

Instead, try to have a nutritious diet with plenty of vegetables and fruits if they are available.

"SLEEP WELL, THINK WELL"[202]

Without enough sleep, it's hard to pay attention, understand new material, and recall previously  learned information. Even if your reasons for cutting down on your sleep are well intentioned, such as to gain more study time, you'll likely have more school problems the following day—not fewer—if you don't get enough sleep.

Moreover, sleeping well gives your brain time to consolidate and store memories of what you learned the previous day.[203] That frees up your brain to take in new information, making the next day's learning easier.[204] Also, during the day, toxins (poisonous substances) build up in your brain. But with enough sleep, they are washed away at night.[205]

If you're having trouble getting to sleep, one reason might be that the blue light from your computer, cell phone, or other device has reduced your body's production of the sleep-inducing hormone, melatonin. *At least* a half hour before going to bed, stop looking at those devices.[206] "Backlit screens send light signals to your brain that say, 'Wake up!' This can make it hard for you to fall asleep."[207] You also can activate the blue-light filter setting on your cell phone or download a similar computer app.

If you are a teenager, another reason for inadequate sleep could relate to your body's *circadian rhythm*, which reflects 24-hour cycles in your brain and body that heavily influence when you are ready to sleep. For different ages and individuals, that "when" varies. Although most adults may get sleepy at around 10 p.m., often "a few more hours must pass before the circadian rhythm of a teenage brain begins to shut down alertness and allow for easy, sound sleep to begin."[208] Then, because of early school start times, the alarm goes off before the teenager had enough sleep. If you're pretty young, do the best you can, and support any efforts to schedule later school start times.

CONCLUSION. Without further delving into why a healthy lifestyle is so important for effective learning, it suffices to say that to maximize your ability to learn, you need adequate sleep, exercise, and a good diet. These are "the three foundations upon which your brain health is built."[209] Also seek to reduce stress and its harmful effects on your brain and focus.

APPENDIX C
USE ABBREVIATIONS FOR FASTER WRITING

Below are some abbreviations and symbols for faster note taking. You can add your own, as long as you use them consistently. You'll have some for particular subjects—such as WWII (World War II) in history.[210]

	ABBREVIATIONS		SYMBOLS
amt	amount	w/	with
b/c	because	w/o	without
b4	before	±	about, more or less
bk.	book	&	and
b/t	between	8	words ending in "ate"
ch.	chapter	4	for
chem	chemical	2	to, too, two
diff	different, difference	Δ	change
econ	economics, economy	"	same as above, ditto
e.g.	for example	=	equal
Eng	English	≠	unequal
esp.	especially	≈	approximately
etc.	and so on	>	greater than
govt	government	<	less than
incl	including, includes	≥	= to or greater than
info	information	≤	= to or less than
p.	page (pp. = pages)	#	number
para	paragraph	%	percent, percentage
re	regarding, about	+	plus, more
sect	section	∴	therefore
s/t	something,	↑	increase
subj	subject	↓	decrease
vs	versus, against	X	no, incorrect
yr.	year	/	per (50 mi./gal.)

ACKNOWLEDGEMENTS

First, I'd like to thank my editor, Kerri Landis, for his incredible work. Although he is a Reedsy editor I never met, my feeling throughout the editing process was that he was an old friend who happened to be a highly skilled editor who was doing everything possible to make my book a success. He understood what I was trying to communicate, and I felt that he was rooting for me. His high level of effort remained the same from the first page to the last, and he had eagle eyes for spotting where corrections and improvements could be made. He also contributed valuable style and formatting suggestions, and generally made this a much better book.

I'd also like to thank ahmedfani of Fiverr International Ltd for his skill and creativity in drawing most of this book's illustrations.

Finally I want to express my gratitude to my bibliography. Yes, that's an unorthodox acknowledgement, but I'd like to highlight the fact that I couldn't have written this book a couple of decades ago. It has only been possible because of the tremendous amount of outstanding, recent thinking and research that has taken place about the learning process. I'm totally in debt to the authors who did this work and published their findings.

For questions, concerns, or a free teaching guide,
email effectivelearning9@gmail.com

BIBLIOGRAPHY

Adler, Mortimer J. and Van Doren, Charles. *How to Read a Book: The Classical Guide to Intelligent Reading.* New York: Touchstone, 1972.

Ahrens, Sönke. *How to Take Smart Notes: One Simple Technique to Boost Writing, Learning and Thinking – for Students, Academics and Nonfiction Book Writers.* Middletown, DE: Sönke Ahrens (takesmartnotes.com), 2017.

Amen, Daniel G. *Change Your Brain, Change Your Grades.* Dallas, TX: BenBella Books, Inc, 2019.

Bailey, Francis and Pransky, Ken. *Memory at Work in the Classroom: Strategies to Help Underachieving Students.* Alexandria, VA: ASCD, 2014.

Baker, Michael. *The Basics of Critical Thinking.* North Bend, OR: The Critical Thinking Co., 2015.

Bathla, Som. *Intelligent Thinking: Overcoming Thinking Errors, Learn Advanced Techniques to Think Intelligently, Make Smarter Choices, and Become the Best Version of Yourself.* sombathla@gmail.com. Kindle ed.

Boser, Ulrich. *Learn Better: Mastering the Skills for Success in Life, Business, and School, or, How to Become an Expert in Just About Anything.* New York: Rodale Wellness, 2017.

Brown, Peter C., Roediger III, Henry L., and McDaniel, Mark A. *Make It Stick: The Science of Successful Learning.* Cambridge, MA: The Belknap Press, 2014.

Brown, Sunni. *The Doodle Revolution: Unlock the Power to Think Differently.* New York: Portfolio/Penguin, 2014.

Buckley, Susan, editor. *Build Our Nation: American History and Geography.* Boston, Houghton Mifflin, 2003

Burger, Edward B. and Starbird, Michael. *The 5 Elements of Effective Thinking.* Princeton, NJ: Princeton University Press, 2012.

Butler, David. *Reading with the Right Brain: Read Faster by Reading Ideas Instead of Just Words.* Publisher: Author, 2014.

Buzan, Tony and Buzan, Barry. *Mind Map Book: How to Use Radiant Thinking to Maximize You Brain's Untapped Potential.* New York: Plume, 1996.

Carey, Benedict. *How We Learn: The Surprising Truth About When, Where, and Why It Happens.* New York: Random House, 2014.

Carter, Nichole. *Sketchnoting in the Classroom: A Practical Guide to Deepen Student Learning*. Portland, OR: International Society for technology in Education, 2019.

Carter, Rita, et. al. *The Human Brain Book*. 3rd ed. New York: Dorling, Kindersley Limited (DK) Division of Penguin Random House, 2019.

Claxton, Guy. *Hare Brain Tortoise Mind: Why Intelligence Increases When You Think Less*. London: Fourth Estate, Paperback Edition, 1998.

Clear, James. *Atomic Habits: An Easy & Proven Way to Build Good Habits & Break Bad Ones.* New York: Avery Imprint of Penguin Random House, 2018.

Coleman, Daniel. *Emotional Intelligence* (tenth anniversary ed.). New York: Bantam Dell, 2006.

Crossman, Anne. *Study Smart, Study Less*. Berkeley, CA: Ten Speed Press, 2011.

Davis, Leslie and Sirotowitz, Sandi, with Parker, Harvey C. *Study Strategies Made Easy: A Practical Plan for School Success*. Plantation, FL: Specialty Press, 2012.

De Bono, Edward. *Intelligence, Information, Thinking*. Dublin, Ireland: Blackhall Publishing, 2007.

De Bono. *Teach Your Child How to Think*. New York: Penguin Books, 1992.

Dehaene, Stanislas. *How We Learn: Why Brains Learn Better Than Any Machine for Now*. New York: Penguin Books, 2020.

Dellis, Nelson (author) and Stillwell, Seph (illustrator). M*emory Super-Powers: An Adventurous Guide to Remembering What You Don't Want to Forget*. New York: Abrams Books, 2020.

Dirksen, Julie. Design for How People Learn. 2nd ed. San Francisco, CA: New Riders, 2016.

Doyle, Terry and Zakrajsek. *The New Science of Learning: How to Learn in Harmony with Your Brain.* Sterling, VA: Stylus, 2013.

Duckworth, Angel. *Grit: The Power of Passion and Perseverance.* New York: Scribner, 2016.

Dweck, Carol S. *Mindset: the new psychology of success*. New York: Ballantine Books, 2008.

Elliot, Andrea. *Invisible Child: Poverty, Survival, and Hope in an American City.* [Audiobook, narrated by Adenrele Ojo] New York: Penguin Random House, 2021.

Emdin, Christopher. *For White Folks Who Teach in the Hood and the rest of y'all too.* Boston, MA: Beacon Press, 2016.

Ericsson, Anders and Pool, Robert. *Peak: Secrets from the New Science of Expertise.* New York: Houghton Mifflin Harcourt, 2016.

Farndon, John. *1000 Facts on Science and Technology.* New York: Barnes & Noble Books, 2001.

Firth, Jonathan. *How to Learn: Effective study and revision methods for any course.* Middletown, DE: Arboretum Books, 2018.

Flores, Gloria P. *Learning to Learn and the Navigation of Moods: The Meta-Skill for the Acquisition of Skills.* Gloria P. Flores, 2016.

Foer, Joshua. *Moonwalking with Einstein: The Art and Science of Remembering Everything.* The Penguin Group: New York, 2011.

Forsten, Char. *Teaching Thinking and Problem Solving in Math.* Scholastic Professional Books: New York, 1992.

Frender, Gloria. *Learning to Learn: Strengthening Study Skills and Brain Power.* Chicago, IL: World Book, Inc./Incentive Publications, 2014.

Fried, Robert L. *The Game of School: Why We All Play It, How It Hurts Kids, and What It Will Take to Change It.* San Francisco, CA: Jossey-Bass, 2005.

Frank, Thomas. *10 Steps to Earning Awesome Grades (while studying less).* Copyright 2015 Thomas Frank

Fry, Ron. *How to Study, 7th Ed.* Boston, MA: Course Technology, 2101.

Gallo, Michael A. and Kiehl, Charles F. Introductory Algebra. St. Paul, MN: West Publishing Company, 1985.

Gates, Bill and Melinda. "Educating America's Young People for the Global Economy." In *Waiting for Superman: How We Can Save America's Failing Public Schools*, edited by Karl Weber. New York: Public Affairs, 2010: 201-212.

Gaugler, Vincent H. *How to Study and Get Good Better Best Grades.* Camarillo, CA: Xulon Press, 2010.

Gelb, Michael J. *How to Think like Leonardo da Vinci: Seven Steps to Genius Every Day*. New York: Delacorte Press, 1998.

Grandin, Temple. *Visual Thinking: The Hidden Gifts of People who Think in Pictures, Patterns, and Abstractions*. New York: Riverhead Books, 2022.

Grant, Adam. *Think Again: The Power of Knowing What You Don't Know*. New York: Viking, an imprint of Penguin Random House, 2021. Audiobook.

Green, Gordon W., Jr. *Getting Straight A's*. Secaucus, NJ: Lyle Stuart Inc. 1985.

Greenberg, Michael. *Painless Study Techniques*. Huappauge, NY: Barron's Educational Series, Inc., 2009.

Haber, Jonathan. *Critical Thinking*. Cambridge, MA: The MIT Press, 2020.

Hardiman, Mariale, M. *Connecting Brain Research with Effective Teaching: The Brain-Targeted Teaching Model*. Lantham, MD: Rowman & Littlefield Education, 2003.

Hari, Johann. *Stolen Focus: Why You Can't Pay Attention—and How to Think Deeply Again*. New York: Random House Audio, 2022.

Higbee, Kenneth L. *Your Memory: How It Works & How to Improve It, 2nd ed.* Cambridge, MA: Da Capo Press, 2001.

Hollins, Peter. *The Science of Self-Learning: How to Teach Yourself Anything, Learn More in Less Time, and Direct Your Own Education*. Middletown, DE: Peter Hollins, 2019.

Hoover, Gary. *The Lifetime Learner's Guide to Reading and Learning*. Philadelphia, PA: Assiduity Publishing House, 2017.

Horsely, Kevin. *Unlimited Memory: How to Use Advanced Learning Strategies to Learn Faster, Remember More, and Be More Productive*. Granger, IN: TCK Publishing.com, 2016.

Hubbard, L. Ron. *Study Skills for Life*. St. Louis, MO: Effective Education Publishing, 2004.

Jack, Anthony Abraham. *The Privileged Poor: How Elite Colleges Are Failing Disadvantaged Students*. Narrated by Mirron Willis. Tantor Media, Inc. 2019. Audiobook.

Jensen, Eric. *Teaching with the Brain in Mind*, 2nd ed. Alexandria, VA: ASCD, 2005.

Kahneman, Daniel. *Thinking, Fast and Slow*. New York: Farrar, Straus and Giroux, 2011.

Jones, Kate. *Retrieval Practice: Research & Resources for every classroom*. Melton, England, John Cart Educational, Ltd., 2019.

Koomey, Jonathan G. *Turning Numbers into Knowledge: Mastering the Art of Problem Solving*. 2nd ed. Oakland, CA: Analytics Press, 2010.

Kornhauser, Arthur W. Revised by Diane M. Enerson. How to Study: Suggestions for High School & College Students. 3rd ed. Chicago, IL: The University of Chicago Press, 1993.

Kundu, Anindya. *The Power of Student Agency: Looking Beyond Grit to Close the Opportunity Gap*. Narrated by Neil Shah. TantorMedia, Inc.,2021. Audio.

Kwik, Jim. *Limitless: Upgrade Your Brain, Learn Anything Faster, and Unlock Your Exceptional Life*. Carlsbad, CA: Hay House, Inc., 2020.

Lahart, Stephanie (2013). *Teens Matter Most: A Powerful, Straightforward Guide for Teens. Your life has purpose, and you are important* [Kindle edition]. Retrieved from amazon.com on 11/26/2020.

Lang, James M. *Small Teaching: Everyday Lessons from the Science of Learning.* San Francisco, CA: Jossey-Bass, 2016.

Langer, Ellen J. *The Power of Mindful Learning.* Boston, MA: Da Capo Press, 2016.

Lavoie, Richard. *The Motivation Breakthrough: 6 Secret to Turning on the Tuned-Out Child*. New York: Touchstone (a Division of Simon & Shuster, Inc.), 2007.

Learning Express. *Reading Comprehension Success in 20 Minutes a Day (6th ed.)*. New York: Learning Express, 2016.

Leslie, Kadeem. *The Full Student: How I Run a Six Figure Business and Still Get Straight A's.* Middletown, DE: Kadeem Leslie, 2020.

Levy, Jonathan A. *The Only Skill That Matters: The Proven Methodology to Read Faster, Remember More, and Become a Superlearner*. Austin, TX: Lioncrest Publishers, 2019.

Lorayne, Harry and Lucas, Jerry. The *Memory Book*. New York: Ballantine Books, 1974.

Lucas, Jerry. *Learning How to Learn: The Ultimate Learning and Memory Instruction.* Dallas, TX: Lucas Educational Systems, Inc., 2001.

Lucas, Jerry. *Picture Perfect Spanish.* Dallas, TX: Lucas Educational Systems, Inc., 2000.

McCabe, Bret. (Breaking) Bad Teacher. Johns Hopkins Magazine, Vol. 65 No. 1, Fall 2013:24-25.

McGuire, Saundra Yancy, with McGuire, Stephanie. *Teach Yourself How to Learn: Strategies You Can Use to Ace Any Course at Any Level.* Sterling, VA: Stylus Publishing, LLC, 2018

McPherson, Fiona. *Effective Notetaking (2nd ed.).* Wellington, New Zealand: Wayz Press, 2007.

McTighe, Jay and Silver, Harvey F. *Teaching for Deeper Meaning: Tools to Engages Students in Meaning Making.* Alexandria, VA:ASCD, 2020.

Medina, John. *Brain Rules: 12 Principles for Surviving and Thriving at Work, Home, and School.* Seattle, WA: Pear Press, 2008.

Menakem, Resmaa. *My Grandmother's Hands: Racialized Trauma and the Pathway to Mending Our Hears and Bodies.* Las Vegas, NV: Central Recovery Press, 2017.

Metha, Jal and Fine, Sarah. *In Search of Deeper Learning: The Quest to Remake the American High School.* Cambridge, MA: Harvard University Press, 2019.

Metivier, Anthony. *How to Learn & Memorize Math, Numbers, & Simple Arithmetic.* Middletown, DE: Metivier Magnetic Memory Series, 2021.

Michalko, Michael. *Cracking Creativity: The Secrets of Creative Genius.* Berkeley CA: Ten Speed Press, 2001.

Milkman, Katy. *How to Change: The Science of Getting from Where You Are to Where You Want to Be.* London: Vermillion, 2021.

Mills, Emily. *The Art of Visual Notetaking: An Interactive Guide to Visual Communication and Sketchnoting.* Mission Viejo, CA: Walter Foster Publishing, 2019.

Muchnick, Cynthia Clumeck. *The Everything Guide to Study Skills: Strategies, Tips, and Tools You Need to Succeed in School!.* Avon, MA: Adams Media, 2011.

National Research Council. *How People Learn: Brian, Mind, Experience, and School.* Expanded Edition. Washington, DC: The National Academies Press, 2000.

Newport, Cal. *How to Be a High School Superstar: A Revolutionary Plan to Get into College by Standing Out (Without Burning*

Newport, Cal. *How to Become a Straight-A Student: The Unconventional Strategies Real College Students Use to Score High While Studying Less.* New York: Three Rivers Press, 2007.

Oakley, Barbara. *A Mind for Numbers: How to Excel at Math and Science (Even If You Flunked Algebra).* New York: Penguin Group: 2014.

Oakley, Barbara. *Mindshift: Break Through Obstacles to Learning and Discover Your Hidden Potential.* New York: Penguin Random House LLC, 2017.

Oakley, Barbara, Rogowsky & Sejnowski. *Uncommon Sense Teaching: Practical Insights in Brain Science to Help Students Learn.* New York: tarcher perigee, 2021.

Oakley, Barbara and Sejnowski, Terrence. *Learning How to Learn: A Guide for Kids and Teens.* New York: tarcher perigee, 2018.

O'Brien, Dominic. *How to Develop a Brilliant Memory Week by Week: 52 Proven Ways to Enhance Your Memory.* London: Watkins Media Limited, 2015.

O'Brien, Dominic. *How to Pass Exams.* London: Watkins Media Limited, 2015.

O'Conner, Patricia T. *Woe Is I: The Grammarphobe's Guide to Better English in Plain English.* 3rd ed. New York: Riverhead Books, 2009.

Orwell, Nathan. *Medical Terminology: An Easy and Practical Way to Better Understand, Pronounce, and Memorize Medical Terms.* Middleton, DE: Nathan Orwell, 2022.

Østby, Hilde & Østby, Ylva. *Adventures in Memory: The Science and Secrets of Remembering and Forgetting.* Translated by Marianne Lindvale. Vancouver: Greystone Books, 2018.

Paul, Annie Murphy. *The Extended Mind: The Power of Thinking Outside the Brain.* Boston and New York: Mariner Books, 2021.

Penn, Paul. *The Psychology of Effective Studying: How to Succeed in Your Degree.* New York: Routledge, 2010.

Phillips, Emily Krone. *The Make-or-Break Year: Solving the Dropout Crisis One Ninth Grader at a Time.* New York: The New Press, 2019.

Restack, Richard. *Optimizing Brain Fitness.* The Great Courses series. Chantilly, VA: The Teaching Company, 2122.

Ripley, Amanda. *The smartest kids in the world and how they got that way*. New York: Simon & Shuster, 2013.

Ritchhart, Ron; Church, Mark; Morrison, Karin. *Making Thinking Visible: How to promote Engagement, Understanding, and Independence for All Learners*. San Francisco, CA: Jossey-Bass, 2011.

Rhodes, Matthew G.; Cleary, Anne M.; and DeLosh, Edward L. *A Guide to Effective Studying and Learning: Practical Strategies from the Science of Learning*. New York; Oxford University Press, 2020.

Robinson, Adam. *What Smart Students Know: Maximum Grades, Optimum Learning, Minimum Time*. New York: Three Rivers Press, 1993.

Seeley, Cathy L. *Making Sense of Math: How to Help Every Student Become a Mathematical Thinker and Problem Solver*. Alexandria, VA: ASCD Publications, 2016.

Sesno, Frank. *Ask Questions: The Power of Questions to Open Doors, Uncover Solutions, and Spark Change*. New York: AMACON, 2017.

Sirotowitz, Sandi; Davis., Leslie; Parker, Harvey. *Study Strategies Plus: Building Your Study Skills and Executive Functioning for School Success*. Plantation, FL: Specialty Press, Inc., 2012.

Sousa, David A. *How the Brain Learns (5th ed.)*. Thousand Oaks, CA: Corwin, a Sage Publishing Company, 2017.

Tileston, Donna Walker and Darling, Sandra K. *Why Culture Counts: Teaching Children of Poverty*. Bloomington, IN: Solution Tree Press, 2008.

Tough, Paul. *Helping Children Succeed: What Works and Why*. Mariner Books, Houghton Mifflin Harcourt, 2016

Tough, Paul. *How Children Succeed: Grit, Curiosity, and the Hidden Power of Character*. New York: Houghton Mifflin Harcourt Publishing Company, 2012.

Turgeon, Heather & Wright, Julie, "We're ignoring a major culprit behind the teen mental health crisis," *The Washington Post*, 22 May 2022, p. A27.

Van Der Kolk, Bessel. *The Body Keeps Score: Brain, Mind, and Body in the Healing of Trauma*.   New York: Penguin Books, 2014.

Walker, Matthew. *Why We Sleep: The New Science of Sleep and Dreams*. New York: Penguin Random House, 2017.

Webster's II New Riverside University Dictionary, 1984.

Westover, Tara. *Educated: A Memoir*. New York: Random House, 2018.

White, Ron. *Memory Improvement: How to Improve Your Memory in Just 30 Days.* Melrose, FL: Laurenzana Press, 2010-2013.

Wiederman, Michael W. *Study Less, Learn More: The Complete Guide for Busy Students*. Columbia, SC: Mindful Publications, LLC, 2013.

Willingham, Daniel T. *Outsmart Your Brain: Why Learning Is Hard and How You Can Make It Easy.* New York: Gallery Books, 2023.

Willingham, Daniel T. *Why Don't Students Like School? A Cognitive Scientist Answers Questions About How the Mind Works and What It means For the Classroom.* San Francisco: Jossey-Bass, A Wiley Imprint, 2009

Wilson, John. *Thinking with Concepts*. Cambridge, England: Cambridge University Press, 1963.

Wooden, John and Yaeger, Don. *A Game Plan for Life: The Power of Mentoring.* New York: Bloomsbury, 2009.

Zimmermann, Susan and Hutchins, Chryse. *7 Keys to Comprehension: How to Help Your Kids Read It and Get It*. New York: Three Rivers Press, 2003.

Zull, James E. *From Brain to Mind: Using Neuroscience to Guide Change in Education*. Sterling, VA: Stylus Publishing, LLC, 2011.

ENDNOTES

[1] Kwik, p. 41. See also Rhodes, Cleary, and DeLosh, p. 13.

[2] Newport (2007), p. 4.

[3] Lahart, pp. 9, 45-46.

[4] The paragraph and the idea are from Beilock, pp. 235-237.

[5] Fry, p. 46.

[6] Butler, pp. 123-24; Ambrose, et al., pp. 121-130; McGuire, p.42.

[7] Robinson, p. 57.

[8] Burger & Starbird, p. 74.

[9] Amen, p. 96; Levi, pp. 126-127.

[10] McTighe & Silver, p. 58. See also Adler & Van Doren, pp. 32-36; Robinson, pp. 53-55; Kruger, p. 66, Hoover, pp. 11-15, 104; Hollins, pp. 47-52; Levi, p. 121-122, and Oakley (2014), p. 11.

[11] Levi, p. 125.

[12] Ahrens, p. 88.

[13] McPherson, p. 12.

[14] Kornhauser, pp. 29-30.

[15] Tovani (2004), pp. 68-70, 73; Frank, p. 40.

[16] Penn, pp. 63-64.

[17] McTighe & Silver, pp. 13-27.

[18] Ahrens, p. 118 quoting Charlie Munger, an American investor and businessman.

[19] Bathla, location 884.

[20] Bathla, ch. 3, para 1.

[21] Amen, p. 79.

[22] McGuire, p. 29.

[23] Ahrens, p. 86. "…While writing down an idea feels like a detour, extra time spent not writing it down is the real waste of time, as it renders most of what we read as ineffectual."

[24] Buzan, p. 39.

[25] Ahrens, p. 54. Also see pp. 85-86, 94.

[26] Buzan, p. 43.

[27] McTighe & Silver, p. 29.

[28] Kwik, p. 205.

[29] McPherson, p. 6.

[30] Boser, p.113.

[31] Willingham (2023), p. 110.
[32] Frank, pp. 25-28.
[33] Bathla, location 1163. See also Kwik, p. 207; Oakley, Rogowsky & Sejnowski, p. 144; Ahrens, p.78.; and Leslie, p. 62.
[34] Willingham (2023), pp. 35-37
[35] Buzan, p. 101; Robinson, p. 91.
[36] Michalko, p. 51.
[37] Boser, p. 122; Gelb, pp. 165-189; Buzan, pp. 39-41; Michalko (2001), pp. 53-80.
[38] McPherson, p. 177.
[39] Brown, Sunni, pp. 112-13, 16-117.
[40] Amen, pp. 110-111.
[41] Willingham (2023), P. 13.
[42] Sirotowitz, Davis, and Parker, pp.117-121.
[43] Amen, p. 113.
[44] Newport (2007), p. 16.
[45] Sousa, pp. 33-35.
[46] Wiederman, p. 28. See also Østby & Østby, pp. 194-195.
[47] Medina, p. 87.
[48] Leslie, pp41-42.
[49] Horsley, p. 18.
[50] Jones, p. 147. See also Rhodes, Cleary, and DeLosh, p. 136.
[51] Hari, entire book.
[52] Crossman, p. 23; Amen, p. 67.
[53] Kruger, p. 49; Emdin. p. 114.; Amen, p 68, Ahrens, pp. 58-60.
[54] Paul, pp. 122-123.
[55] Crossman, p. 24.
[56] Brown, Sunni, p. 115. See also Willingham (2023), pp. 241-242.
[57] Leslie, pp. 23-39.
[58] Kornhauser, pp. 15-16.
[59] Zull, pp. 195, 259.
[60] Leslie, p. 50.
[61] Kornhauser, p. 14.
[62] Kwik, p. 48 suggests 25 minutes on average. See also Horsely, p. 107, who recommends breaks every 35-40 minutes, and O'Brien (How to Pass Exams), p.236 who suggests short bursts of 20

minutes, and Willingham (2016), p. 223 who recommends 20-60 minutes.

[63] Jensen, pp. 45-46; Levi, pp. 174-175; Oakley, Rogowski & Sejnowski, p 52.

[64] Paul, p. 52.

[65] Ahrens, p. 73.

[66] Amen, pp.68-69.

[67] Oakley & Sejnowski, pp. 32-38; Sousa, pp. 139-140; Hollins, pp. 108-109; Penn, pp. 35-36; Newport (2017), pp. 15-17. (If you're in college or soon will be, Newport's book is must-read.)

[68] Oakley (2014), p. 17, where she describes the Einstellung effect.

[69] Michalko, pp. 114-115.

[70] Michalko, pp. 2, 114-115, 154, 168, 247.

[71] Thinking in terms of high and low focus modes was inspired by discussions of the diffuse (or relaxed) mode in Oakley (2014), ch. 2; Oakley (2017), pp. 115-125; and Oakley & Sejnowski, ch.2; and by Claxton, entire book (which uses deliberative mode for hifoc and various terms for the relaxed, lofoc mode). Jensen , p. 132 states that "An item in working memory usually lasts for 5 to 30 seconds before either disappearing or being reactivated." See also Claxton, p. 9.

[72] Dehaene, p. 16.

[73] Oakley (2014), pp.9-28; Rhodes, Cleary ; and DeLosh, p. 229.

[74] Rhodes, Cleary, and DeLosh, p.229; Carter, p. 170 ("When the brain defocuses, information flows more freely around its highways of connecting fibers.").

[75] Medina, p. 152; Michalko, *Cracking*, pp. 107-110; Hardiman, pp. 47-48.

[76] Leslie, p. 154-164.

[77] For more details on this approach, see Kruger, pp. 39-44.

[78] Schedule-formats resemble those in Shao and Jagan and Frender, p. 51.

[79] Frank, pp. 55-60; Willingham (2023), p. 194.

[80] Oakley (2014), *p.* 43.

[81] Boser, p. 88. Also, Jones, p. 41. Both referenced Graham Hill's *The Hidden Lives of Learners*.

[82] Dehaene, pp. 216-220. "Immediately after reading our textbook or our class notes, information is fully present in our mind. It sits in or conscience working memory, in an active form. We feel as if we know it, because it is present in our short-term storage space, but this short-term compartment has nothing to do with long-term memory that we will need in order to retrieve the same information a few days later."

[83] Brown, et al., pp. 3, 15, 74; Rhodes, Cleary, and DeLosh, pp. 69, 89, 95-98, 156.

[84] Oakley, Rogowsky & Sejnowski, p. 8. For a book-length explanation of retrieval practice, see Jones.

[85] Wiederman, pp. 57-59.

[86] Ahrens, pp. 85-87.

[87] Doyle & Zakrajsek, p. 75. See also Penn, 205-209.

[88] For more on schedules and motivation, see Kahneman, pp. 40-44.

[89] Dweck, pp. 227-228; Boser, pp. 66, 101.

[90] Koomey, p. 34.

[91] Firth, p. 35.

[92] Foer, p. 48.

[93] Lang, pp. 14-15.

[94] Higbee, pp. 215-217.

[95] Kwik, p. 215.

[96] O'Brien (How to Develop a Brilliant Memory), p. 24.

[97] Horsely, p. 61.

[98] Lucas (2000), p. 206.

[99] Medina, pp. 128-130.

[100] The "hook" terminology is from Robinson, especially pp. 112-119.

[101] Medina, p. 114.

[102] Rhodes, Cleary, and DeLosh, p. 195.

[103] Robinson, p. 112.

[104] Dehaene, pp. 206-209. When the auditory area of your brain keeps getting the expected message, responses from that area progressively decrease.

[105] Østby & Østby, pp. 169-170.

[106] Ahrens, p. 105.

[107] Willingham (2023), pp. 118-120.

[108] Sirotowitz, Davis, and Parker, p. 127.

[109] Ali, p. 84.   Also can be written as Area = ba/2, but the hook doesn't work as well.

[110] Metivier, p. 137 as told to the author by math expert Robert Ahdoot.

[111] Foer, p. 91.

[112] Levy, p. 79.

[113] Horsley, pp. 28-29.

[114] Echeverria, pp. 8-10, 22-23.

[115] Most of the Memory Palace/Loci/Journey Method material reflects Higbee, pp. 144-156. See also Levi, pp. 91-104; Horsely, pp. 53-60; and O'Brien (How to Develop…), pp. 77-87.

[116] Tileston & Darling, pp. 64, 83. See also Dehaene, p185.

[117] Dellis, pp129-130.

[118] Kwik, p. 66. See also Medina, pp. 171-172.

[119] Dweck. Entire book focuses on these ideas.

[120] Dweck, pp 5-11, 39-41.

[121] Brown, et al, pp.179-183; Dweck, p. 219.

[122] Zull, p. 155; Bathla, location 389.

[123] Jensen, pp. 11-12.

[124] Jbar, Ferris. Scientific American: "Cache Cab: Taxi Drivers' Brains Grow to Navigate London's Streets." 12/8/2011.   See also Kwik, pp. 36-37 and Østby & Østby, pp.152-159.

[125] Ericsson & Pool, pp. xvi -xvii, 45, 223.

[126] Dweck, p. 219.

[127] Goleman, pp. 86-88.

[128] Cited in Penn, p. 18.

[129] Lovoie, p. 92.

[130] Tovani (2004), p. 103.

[131] Bailey & Pransky, especially pp. 128-185.

[132] Dehaene, p. 142.

[133] Ripley, pp. 116-118. See also Dehaene, pp. 199-201.

[134] Tough (2012), pp. 85-86.

[135] Milkman, p. 164.

[136] Boser, pp. 95-96.

[137] Cited in Burger & Starbird, p. 50. Similarly, "after losing a big game in the 2016 NBA finals, LeBron James almost immediately began reviewing the tape of the game. 'I'll figure out ways I can be better, starting as soon as I leave this podium,' James said." Cited in Boser, p. 201.
[138] Dweck, pp. 85-86.
[139] Robinson, p. 21.
[140] Boser p. 47.
[141] Sousa, 164.
[142] Østby & Østby, p.26.
[143] Willingham (2009), p. 37.
[144] Oakley, Rogowsky & Sejnowski, p. 24.
[145] Willingham (2009), pp. 42-44.
[146] Willingham (2009), pp.169-187.
[147] Flores. pp. 26-30 and rest of the book.
[148] Oakley, Rogowsky & Sejnowski, p. 76.
[149] Kwik, p. 81.
[150] Hollins, pp. 168-169.
[151] Amen, pp. 174-175.
[152] Greenberg, p. 157.
[153] For more detailed instructions, see Robinson, pp. 185-200.
[154] Firth, pp. 66-67.
[155] Green, pp. 65-66.
[156] Green, pp. 68-69, 143-144.
[157] Green, pp. 3-75.
[158] Willingham (2023), p. 170.
[159] Goleman, p. 84. See also Weiderman, pp. 104-106 and Østby & Østby , pp. 199-200.
[160] Amen, p. 158.
[161] Learning Express, p. 203.
[162] Leslie, p. 72.
[163] Quote from Vince Lombardi, former coach of the Green Bay Packers football team.
[164] Duckworth, ch. 8.
[165] Milkman, pp. 109-112 on the advantage of breaking down big goals into more easily achievable bite-size chunks.
[166] Clear, pp. 15-23.

167 Webster's, p. 683.

168 Carter, R., p. 157.

169 Carter, R., p. 70. Although neurons are involved with most of the thinking in the brain, and that's sufficient for this simplified explanation, there are other varieties of cells that assist the neurons carry out thinking and remembering. See " The other brain cells," *The Economist*, 28 Jan 2023, 71-72.

170 Jensen, p. 17; Sousa, p. 22; Carter, pp. 71-73.

171 For a more expert, better illustrated explanation, see Oakley & Sejnowski, ch. 4. and Oakley, Rogowsky & Sejnowski, p. 4.

172 Jensen, p. 18, Claxton, pp. 135-245.

173 Dehaene, pp. 89-90; Østby & Østby, p. 19.

174 Østby & Østby , p. 24. "Memories seldom swim around without connections, like a lonesome fish. Instead, they are caught in a fishing net full of other memories. When you want to recall a memory, you have a greater chance at catching it if you scoop up the other memories around it)

175 Sousa, p. 88.

177 Jensen, p. 16; Carter, pp. 160-161.

178 Oakley, Rogowsky & Sejnowski, pp. 74-75.

179 Higbee, p. 19—"Information stored in short-term memory is forgotten in less than 30 second"; Amen, pp. 117-119—puts the time it lasts in immediate memory at less than a second. Østby & Østby , p. 7—Regarding learning a new word or somebody name: "These things remain I our memories for no more than a few seconds, or as long as we keep thinking about them."

180 Authoritative sources differ on the capacity of short-term memory. Medina, p. 130—"The typical human brain can hold about **seven** pieces of information for less than 30 seconds!" Higbee, p. 19—"**Seven** items for most people."; Oakley and Sejnowski, p. 92—"**four** but some can have **five or even more**."; Boser. p. 41—"Our brains being able to juggle only **three or four** items at a time."; National Research Council, p. 96—"**Up to seven** items (**between five and nine**, actually), people can readily handle a variety of tasks; with more than seven, they simply can't handle them handily."; Zull, p. 92—"In general we can mentally hold and

manipulate **an average of seven** distinct elements (words, images, numbers, etc.) simultaneously."; Jensen, p.42—"Researchers have found that we can take only **three to seven** chunks of information before we simply overload and begin to miss new incoming data."; Ericsson & Pool, p. 2--"For some it is six items, for others it may be seven or eight, but the limit is **generally about seven** items."

[181] McPherson, 8: "Recent research is now converging on the idea that working memory can only hold **four** items, of which only one is in your 'focus of attention' at any one time." See also Oakley, Rogowsky, & Sejnowski, pp. 7, 20-21.

[182] Østby & Østby , p. 10.

[183] Østby & Østby , p.31.

[184] Boser pp. 91-92.

[185] When neural connections keep getting stimulated, an *engram*, or memory trace, is formed. "The more frequently these neural connections are used, the stronger the engram becomes. Thus, repeated firings among cell's hardware' a memory, strengthening it and making its content easier to retrieve." Hardiman, p. 55.

[186] Medina, pp. 174-175.

[187] Medina, p. 176.

[188] Medina, p. 178. See also Østby & Østby , p. 32, noting that consolidation of memories while sleeping doesn't work well when we're stressed. "The neurons don't fire in the same way."

[189] Tough (2016), p. 15.

[190] Kwik, p. 141.

[191] For more on the nature and effects of trauma see Ven der Holt and also Menakem.

[192] Medina, p. 7.

[193] Doyle and Zakrajsek, p.35.

[194] Oakley, Rogowsky & Sejnowski, pp.60-61. "When you exercise, your brain makes a chemical called BDNF. That's short for brain-derived neurotrophic factor," which is a great result of exercising. "BDNF makes your new neurons strong and healthy. It protects them from injury and makes them more likely to connect with other neurons. It also acts like a food for synapses and dendritic spines, making them grow larger." (Oakley & Sejnowski, pp. 136-137.)

[195] Doyle and Zakrajsek, pp. 37-38.
[196] Oakley & Sejnowski, pp. 136-139, 212.
[197] Kwik, p. 137.
[198] Kwik, p. 130.
[199] Doyle and Zakrajsek, pp. 8-9; Dehaene, pp. 96-98.
[200] Oakley & Sejnowski, p. 138.
[201] Kwik, p. 130.
[202] Medina, p. 149.
[203] Rhodes, Cleary ,and DeLosh, p. 157. For an in-depth explanation, see Dehaene, pp. 224-235.
[204] Doyle and Zakrajsek, p. 18.
[205] Oakley & Sejnowski, pp. 165-167; Levi, pp. 173-174.
[206] Recommendation of the National Sleep Foundation.
[207] Oakley & Sejnowski, p. 168.
[208] Walker, p. 92. Also, pp. 13-23 and 82-95 for the entire paragraph.
[209] Levi, p 178.
[210] The idea for Appendix C and most of the abbreviations are from Davis & Sirotowitz, p. 61.

Milton Keynes UK
Ingram Content Group UK Ltd.
UKHW052245280524
443311UK00008B/156